THE LUMINOUS STONE

WESTERN ESOTERICISM IN CONTEXT III

The Luminous Stone

Lucifer in Western Esotericism

Edited by
MICHAEL HOWARD & DANIEL A. SCHULKE

Images by Hagen von Tulien

THREE HANDS PRESS
2016

Jacket cover image *Garden* and rear cover image
Conqueror Wyrm © copyright Francisco D.
Interior book design and dust jacket design by Joseph Uccello.
Deluxe edition designed by Daniel A. Schulke and James Dunk.

Printed in Canada.

ISBN 978-1-945147-04-3 (softcover)

THREE HANDS PRESS
www.threehandspress.com

CONTENTS

IN DEDICATION TO

THE LIFE AND WORK OF

Michael Howard

1948–2015

ROSA IN SEPULCRO FLORET

Introduction

THE ARCANUM OF the 'fallen angel' Lucifer evokes such concepts as heresy, rebellion, pride, liberation from the bonds of demiurgic oppression, and agency for human evolution. Meaning 'light bearer', Lucifer has, from his earliest origins, been hailed by religious and artistic countercultures as a patron saint of enlightenment—the essential quality embodying overthrow of ignorance and the catalytic, inspired process of revelation. Allied to ancient Gnostic cosmological conceptions as a deliverer from a debased state of First Ignorance, the fallen angel has also found important dominion within occult traditions and philosophy.

Yet outside most occult contexts, Lucifer is commonly conflated with the Christian figure of Satan, or the Devil, a relic of early Christian propagandists eager to repudiate and tarnish rival polytheisms. Ironically, this conflation of deific forms is where Christian dogma and some contemporary forms of Satanism are in agreement. Yet despite the common ground of opposition to an overweening and despotic creator, there stands a great gulf between the concept of the Accuser and that of the Light-bringer. This critical distinction was well elucidated by the Process Church of the Final Judgment, whose tritheistic magical philosophy acknowledged the differing entic powers of Lucifer, Satan and Jehovah. The taxonomic differentiation between tenebrator and illuminator has ancient roots and is historically present in folklore and myth; it has even formed the basis of syncretic Christian divinities such as Saint Lucifer.

As an agent of Transmutation, Lucifer's Alchemical link with the Holy *Lapis* of the Philosophers descends through certain medieval legends of the Holy Grail, wherein the object of the sacred quest was a gemstone fallen from his crown. This stone possessed marvelous virtues: its form was ever-shifting, changing its physical properties, and it was reckoned as a potent reservoir of bodily rejuvenation. Green in color, this Luminous Stone is also linked chromatically with the ancient *Tabula Smaragdina* of Hermes Trismegistus.

In many mystical traditions, Lucifer assumed the feminine forms of Lucina, Lucia and Diana Lucifera. In his guise as the Serpent of Eden, he bestowed a magical philosophy of the Luciferian Woman, she who was not born of the clay, and was therefore especially receptive to the forbidden powers which would render one 'as God.' As a metatext of primordial magical transmission, this narrative is also echoed in the ancient scripture *The Book of Enoch*, where the rebel angels, called Watchers, descended to earth, took human wives, and taught them various arts and magic. The bequest of forbidden angelic power to the First Woman, often magically characterized as Light, forms the basis of illuminist and sex-magical arcana in such occult groups as the Order of the Morning Star, the Cultus Sabbati and the eroto-salvific Christianity promulgated by the heretical French priest, the Abbé Boullan.

As the third volume of the WESTERN ESOTERICISM IN CONTEXT series, *The Luminous Stone* sought to examine some of the lesser-known attributes of the fallen angel sometimes known as the 'most beautiful.' By examining this Light through varying magical prisms, it was our aim to draw out the essence of Illumination as manifest through Lucifer, at a time when such mythic principles are of incalculable applicability to the modern seeker. In so doing, we hope these nine treatises cast forth a ray of light upon this greatly misunderstood and enigmatic figure.

—DANIEL A. SCHULKE AND MICHAEL HOWARD

The Latent Radiance

ILLUMINATION AND CONCEALMENT THROUGH THE CELESTIAL FLAME

Richard Gavin

FROM HIS EMERGENCE in the Book of Isaiah through to the popular conceptions (and misconceptions) that are presently extant, the archangel Lucifer has always been characterized as a bearer of light. The purpose of this essay is to explore exactly what light is being borne by this fallen angel and the nature of the enlightenment that contact with this light begets. In other words, precisely what manner of illumination does the Luciferian fire offer to those who experience its incandescence?

The title of Lucifer proper did not appear until St. Jerome's Latin Vulgate translation of the New and Old Testaments, which emerged in the latter part of the fourth century CE. This entity's original appellation was Shahar (or alternately, Shaher), a name that originated in the ancient Canaanite religion that was practiced by the occupants of the Levant region as far back as the third millennium BCE.[1] The dominant religion perpetuated by the Canaanite peoples was originally a polytheistic faith whose pantheon exhibited the influence of not only the Mesopotamians but also that of the ancient Egyptians.

1 See Maria E. Aubet, *The Phoenicians and the West*, Cambridge University Press, 1987.

Prior to the emergence of Abrahamic faiths, which created a marked shift in the region's dominant religious orientation from its pantheistic origins to an eventual absolute monotheism, there was a period during the Iron Age I (1200–1000 BCE) when the Canaanite faith was in fact a monolatry, meaning that while its adherents believed in the supremacy of a primal godhead they also acknowledged and incorporated into their devotions the existence and influence of many different gods and goddesses. Foremost among these deities was Asherah, the Great Goddess. Although historical records of the early Canaanite culture are relatively scant, many scholars are in agreement that there were a considerable number of Jewish residents in Canaan at that point in time. It is very probable that many of these residents had fled to this region in order to escape the bondage of Egyptian servitude, which was well established under the ruling Dynastic lineages of Egypt.

But even a cursory study of the surviving evidence from this era makes it plain that the impact the Canaanite religion had upon the faith that would eventually become Judaism was both deep and multifaceted. For instance, the worship of the Canaanite Asherah was so interwoven with the Hebrew faith that one finds numerous references to Her in the Old Testament, wherein She is referred to as Queen of Heaven.[2]

While it has often been posited that Asherah was the goddess who gave birth to Shahar, god of the morning star, and his twin Shalim, god of the evening star, the Ugaritic myth *The Gracious and Most Beautiful Gods*, which explains the origins of these divine twins, suggests that they were in fact spawned from a divine tryst between El (supreme masculine god of the ancient Canaanites) and two mortal women. Such an account chimes with the long body of esoteric lore concerning the Watchers or the Fallen Ones, who were said to have grown so infatuated with human females that they mated with them, thus spawning the giant race of Nephilim. The Ugaritic text does reference Asherah specifically, but simply as "the Lady", a goddess of the heavens who nursed both semi-divine forms after their birth.

This myth begs the question: with what did Asherah nourish Shahar and Shalim? As a stellar goddess, it is not too great an assumption to posit that the twin stars of dawn and dusk were nourished with ichor, the luminous and ambrosial liquid essence of immortality known only to the divine and those whom the divine favoured. Bolstered by such a divine diet, coupled with the human quotient of their parentage, one can see how Sha-

2 Jeremiah 44:17–19.

tenet of early Christian Gnosticism. Lucifer's Fall was therein mirrored in humanity's loss of Eden; a punishment that only worsened as humanity become increasingly fixated upon the material realm rather than turning their focus toward the spiritual refinement that was required to forge the long and treacherous road back to the Garden.

But beyond this punitive complexion, the Fall may also be viewed as the bridge that conjoins the firmament of stars to the terra firma. Evidencing this is the fact that the Canaanite myth of Shahar has him being sent to Earth in the form of a lightning bolt, which actually fertilized Mother Earth upon striking her.[5] Here we witness the empyrean fires actually altering the Earth, as opposed to being in its murky thrall. The terra firma is fecundated by an alien fire, a flash of sidereal strangeness that brings new perceptions and new forms into being.

Akin to Shahar's seeding of the Earth with heavenly fire is the myth of Anzû, the monstrous deity of ancient Mesopotamia. Anzû was a lord of the storm who stole the Tablets of Destiny from the vault of heaven in order to obtain power over all gods and deities. Such actions are strongly resonant with the Miltonian Satan, who, in the immortal seventeenth century epic poem declared "Better to reign in Hell, than serve in Heaven."[6]

Elsewhere in *Paradise Lost*, the Fallen Angel describes the infernal realm of Hell as being like a vast furnace:

> *"yet from those flames,*
> *No light, but rather darkness visible"*[7]

The netherworld possessing this kind peculiar radiance, this negative light, is widespread. It can be seen in canonical lore as early as the Book of Job, wherein Hell is described as the place "where the light is as darkness,"[8] and it also permeates traditions like Iranian Sufism, with its Darklight, and various occult sodalities who dedicate some or all of their foci to the Mysteries of the Black Sun.

What is illuminated by this radiant darkness is not the mundane realm, but rather the Underworld, the palace where souls are submerged. Its en-

5 Nigel Jackson and Michael Howard, *The Pillars of Tubal-Cain*, Capall Bann Publishing, 2003, p.59

6 John Milton, *Paradise Lost and Other Poems*, Mentor, 1981, p. 44

7 Ibid, p.38

8 Job 10:22

lightenment is not of the intellect, but of the visionary or poetical sense. Milton's Fallen One mused how the mind is its own place and can make a Heaven of Hell and a Hell of Heaven, thus what is altered by Lucifer's light is not the physical realm but our perceptions of same. Henry Corbin suggests that this form of Gnosis can be had by altering one's orientation from the mundane to the North, which is the source of the Darklight.[9] It is a matter of drawing down power from its living source.

Ancient Egyptians posited that the sun sank nightly into Amenta, the Underworld of the Dead, and then rose again at dawn. Yet during those nocturnal hours, the sun would not die but would instead serve as the fire of the underworld, illuminating the Hidden, the formless. It was in this sense an altogether Other sun. In Greek myth, Orpheus also ventured into the Underworld and experienced visions, but the visionary experience in this regard requires the enflaming of a deeper and altogether outré faculty.

Akin to this luminous Darklight of Sufism, Egyptian Amenta, and the Orpheus myth is the ancient lore of the Mesoamericans. Tezcatlipoca is a god indigenous to the faiths of both the Aztec and the Nahua peoples. Like many 'devils' of global orthodoxies, Tezcatlipoca ruled over cosmic elements that many would likely view as perilous, ominous, or simply unpleasant: storms, the nocturnal sky, discord, winds, obsidian stones, as well as a variety of sorcerous techniques such as scrying. Like Lucifer, who suffered the Fall, and Akephalos, who was headless, Tezcatlipoca's power caused his body to be afflicted. Certain myths depict him as missing a foot.[10]

In Nahua myth, Black Tezcatlipoca was the ruler of the north;[11] the direction from which the radiance of the occulted sun pours forth in waves of emerald.

With the stimulation of the visionary sense, which is integral to Luciferian Gnosis, one's reliance upon the preconceived and the quantified is thereby diminished. The intellect, in other words, recoils from this new celestial radiance. To yoke this anomalous enlightenment requires the employment of different faculties, of perceiving with a sense that lies beyond the five physical senses.

9 Henry Corbin, *The Man of Light in Iranian Sufism*, Omega Publications, 1994.

10 As a study of affliction in relation to the Initiatory process, the following work is highly recommended: *The Afflicted Mirror* by Peter Hamilton-Giles, Three Hands Press, 2013.

11 Guilhem Olivier, *Mockeries and Metamorphoses of an Aztec God.* University of Colorado Press, 2003.

This arcane physiological Gnosis is glyphed in the mythic figure of Akephalos, the Headless One. This angelic entity's earliest surviving documented appearance occurs in a Graeco-Egyptian magical text of exorcism that was first translated into English by Charles Wycliffe Goodwin in 1852.[12] Preserved in the British Museum, this text eventually became known colloquially as the London Parchment 46, and Goodwin's translation of it became an integral part of the Initiatory process of members in the Hermetic Order of the Golden Dawn, where it was Invoked as the bearer of one's inner genius, their Holy Guardian Angel.[13]

Aleister Crowley perpetuated this methodology when he, along with George Cecil Jones, formed a magical sodality that was to serve as the succession of the Golden Dawn, the Argentium Astrum, or Order of the Silver Star. Under the aegis of the A∴A∴, Crowley incorporated the ritual of the Headless One under the title Liber Samekh.[14] This ritual was one that Crowley claimed had aided him in attaining Conversation with his Holy Guardian Angel years earlier when he undertook the performance of the *Book of the Sacred Magic of Abramelin the Mage*, a manual of spiritual and daemonic operation that dates back to the 15th century.[15]

In the opening section of *Liber Samekh*, titled The Oath, we see the Headless (or, as it appears in this ritual, the Bornless) One as the bringer of consciousness that allowed humanity to witness the dualities of nature from a unique third position, one that is neither the male nor the female, the just nor the unjust. From this enlightened position of isolated selfhood, which the Hindus term Atman, one can command, as Crowley phrased it, that "every Spell and Scourge of God may be obedient unto Me."[16]

Samekh is the fifteenth letter of the Hebrew alphabet and its numerical value in Gematria is 60, a value equated with 'Vision.'[17] And according to Bill Heidrick's Hebrew Gematria, 60 is also the number of the "Brilliance" associated with Venus.[18] Here the underlying numerical bind be-

12 Samuel Liddell & MacGregor Mathers, *The Goetia: The Lesser Key of Solomon*, Samuel Weiser Inc., 1995, p. 11.

13 Israel Regardie, *The Golden Dawn*, Llewellyn Publications, 1993, p. 442.

14 Aleister Crowley, *Gems from the Equinox*, New Falcon Publications, 1997, p. 323.

15 See *The Book of the Sacred Magic of Abramelin the Mage*, S.L. MacGregor Mathers (trans.), Dover Publications, 1975.

16 Aleister Crowley, *Gems from the Equinox*, New Falcon Publications, 1997, p. 327.

17 Aleister Crowley, *777 and Other Qabalistic Writings*, Samuel Weiser Inc., 1986.

18 www.billheidrick.com

tween Akephalos and Lucifer is made plain, but further examination of the Headless One yields even further resonances.

The word Akephalos is a Greek adjective that means simply "headless." Beyond the Thelemic interpretations mentioned previously, Akephalos had also been incorporated into various magical and esoteric traditions, dating back to at least the Graeco-Egyptian Papyri (or PGM), which historians estimate as having been written between the Third and Fifth centuries CE.

PGM V. 96-172 reads as follows:

> *I am the headless daimon with my sight in my feet; I am the mighty one who possesses the immortal fire; I am the truth who hates the fact that unjust deeds are done in the world; I am the one who makes the lightning flash and the thunder roll;/ I am the one whose sweat falls upon the earth as rain so that it can inseminate it; I am the one whose mouth burns completely; I am the one who begets and destroys; I am the favour of the Aion; my name is a heart encircled by a serpent; come forth and follow.*[19]

Akephalos as the fiery seeder of the earth, as the possessor of the immortal fire; connections with Lucifer/Shahar abound. Also noteworthy is the reference to Akephalos as the daimon with sight in his feet. Other artistic depictions of the Headless One show him as having eyes in his shoulders, still others have him carrying his head like a mere plaything, a bauble whose utility pales in comparison to the unworldly sight of the celestial flame he wields. Such images evidence a shift in visionary faculty, an irrational form of body-rooted perception that suggests a bypassing of the rational mind. They also create a shocking presence; an unworldly form that forcefully reminds the mortal that the angels may communicate with humanity but they are also wholly Other entities.

The irrational mode of esoteric perception inherent in Akephalos was further elaborated upon in the 1930s by the renowned French philosopher, author and eroticist Georges Bataille. Acéphale was the name given by Bataille to both a public review journal he edited and published, and also to a secret society he founded and of which Bataille was the leader. The journal, which lasted only five issues, was a cultural backlash against the rising tide of fascism that was plaguing Europe at that point in time.

19 Hans Dieter Betz, *The Greek Magical Papyri in Translation, Including the Demotic Spells, Volume 1*, University of Chicago Press, 1996, p.103.

He was disheartened by the ignorance, violence and injustice that he saw increasing throughout the continent, particularly in Germany, where National Socialism was increasing in influence and power. Bataille accused the Third Reich of hijacking and misinterpreting the wise and empowering words of philosophers such as Nietzsche in order to suit their vulgar fascistic aims. Given this, one can wonder if part of the inspiration for Bataille invoking the name of Akephalos with his two-pronged undertaking was to summon the entity who is "the truth" and who "hates the fact that unjust deeds are done in the world." From a historical perspective, apocalyptic theology has a longstanding tradition of the beseeching of deities who return to Earth to deliver a swift and supra-human justice. Such a dynamic is understandable, given that these intelligences are being prayed to by peoples who are living under unjust regimes, suffering oppression or outright genocide.

As far as the inner workings of Bataille's Acéphale society goes, information about its membership and its endeavours was fiercely guarded at the time and therefore details about its specific practices are few. According to Allan Stoekel's Introduction to a selection of Bataille writings from this period, the Acéphale group strove for "the rebirth of myth"[20] and the furtherance of new societal values that Bataille had championed in his public writings, namely "expenditure, risk, loss, sexuality, death."[21]

It is also clear that Bataille was intent upon imbuing the Acéphale group with the Gothic atmospherics that have been so integral to magic and sorcery throughout the ages. The "Acephalic men" gathered in a desolate field and performed rites near an ancient oak that was said to have been struck by lightning. This locality was chosen specifically by Bataille, and its import is twofold. Firstly, the lightning is a symbolic bond to Zu, who struck and fecundated the clay of Earth with celestial fire. But also, the lightning-struck tree is the isolated locale, the Forlorn Place, the locality where few mortals dare to go, particularly after sunset. To do so in act of apostasy against the mores of one's host culture, to shatter one's preconceptions about reality in favour of the Other, the uncertain liminality that can only be apprehended when one overcomes what Bataille himself termed 'the tyranny of the head.'

This usurping of the brain's tyranny is not a matter of dashing intelli-

20 Allan Stoekel (ed.), Georges Bataille, *Visions of Excess: Selected Writings 1927–1939 (Theory and History of Literature Vol. 14)*, University of Minnesota Press, 1985.
21 Ibid.

gence in favour of willful ignorance. It is instead an outward going, pressing past the limitations of one's preconceptions and wishes about the nature of reality. This is the nature of the pain of the Fall. Akephalos's name is 'the heart encircled by a serpent.' Wisdom, which has been borne by the Serpent since time immemorial, is therefore to be found in the deepest passions of the heart, not in the reliance of the intellect.

André Masson's logo for the Acéphale journal aptly symbolizes this revolt. A play upon Leonardo da Vinci's Vitruvian Man, Masson's figure was headless. In one hand he held a flaming heart, in the other a dagger. Stars replaced the nipples on his chest. His intestines were visible through the skin and a human skull stared out from the groin. Even by today's standards this is an arresting image, which only lends credence to the notion of Akephalos, Lucifer or any other form of the angelic light-bearer, as one whose presence is the shock of the timeless, the spear that pierces the clouds of certainty, of fixed reality, of the mere present. Such luminescence is not the familiar light of the sun, nor the man-wrought artificial light which humanity employs to fend off the night. Instead it is what Daniel A. Schulke terms the 'Lux Haeresis,' the Light Heretical.[22] That which the heretical light illumines will invariably unnerve and confound. Such is the nature of the Fallen.

Renowned Bohemian-Austrian poet Rainer Maria Rilke phrased it so aptly[23] in his *Duino Elegies*:

> *'If I cried out*
> *who would hear me among the angelic orders?*
> *And suppose one suddenly*
> *took me to his heart*
> *I would shrivel*
> *I couldn't survive*
> *next to his greater existence.*
> *Beauty is only*
> *the first touch of terror*
> *we can still bear*
> *and it awes us so much*
> *because it so coolly disdains to destroy us.*
> *Every single angel is terrible!'*

22 See *Lux Haeresis*, Daniel A. Schulke, Xoanon, 2011.

23 Rainer Maria Rilke, *Duino Elegies*, David Young (trans.), W. W. Norton & Co., 1978.

Saint Lucifer and the Black Arts

Fredrik Eytzinger

"I see you with six eyes. My two, your two, and the Devil's two."[1]

SAINT LUCY OF Syracuse died a martyr in 304 AD during the Great Prosecution as a consequence of having distributed her dowry among the poor in her town, after which her would-be husband became furious and complained to the city's governor Paschasius. She was condemned to work as a prostitute, but as the persecutors were about to bring her in, she stood immoveable, transfixed to the spot, aided by the powers of her God. When the persecutors returned with bundles of fire wood to set her ablaze, it refused to burn. Finally, she died by the blade, either through decapitation or stabbed in the neck by a dagger. In iconic paintings she is often seen carrying her eyes on a plate in one hand and a sword or a palm branch in the other. Some stories say that her eyes were gouged out by her enemies while others claim that it was done by her own hand as a response to a persistent suitor. Whatever the case, her eyes were upon burial miraculously restored.

In Sweden, the Holy Day of Saint Lucy takes place on December the 13th, called *Luciadagen* (eng: Lucia Day), and the feast surrounding this

1 Rustad, Mary S. (ed., trans.) *The Black Books of Elverum.* Galde Press Inc., 2009, p. 21. From a spell to "Win in judicial proceedings" with the aid of Lucifer.

particular day is still today strong in the entire country; the baking of Lucia saffron buns, lighting candles and preparing for Christmas are all part of tradition, and above all it is a day when the Lucia procession takes place in schools, churches, and public institutions. Despite the profanity of the customs around Christmas, they still carry a spark of the enchanted world. The Lucia procession often consists of a train of maidens dressed in white, carrying candles, walking along their path at a slow pace, as the paragon of solemn contemplation of the darkness inside and outside. They walk together with male participants dressed as Staffan Stalledräng (eng: Stephen Stableman) who wear white gowns, cone hats adorned with stars, and they are often seen carrying a large golden star in their hands; an embodiment of Saint Stephen, the first Christian martyr. In the lead walks Lucia with a red ribbon around her waist, palms joined together by the chest, she carries a wreath of leaves on her head adorned with white candles and she brings light into the world in the darkest hours of the year. During the procession the maids and stablemen sing traditional winter hymns while Lucia, at least in modern times, almost always remains silent. But the Lucia commemorated on the 13th of December has little to do with the Christian saint who died a martyr and it is not by coincidence that her celebratory day inaugurates both the magically auspicious and dangerous eleven days before Christmas in Scandinavian folklore.[2] Through her common image, as a light-bringer during times of darkness, she embodies several aspects of pagan and magical belief, and the celebration in its modern form is not much older than a couple of hundred years.

Some would trace her roots to the German female goddess Perchta/Bärta, related to the Swedish word *bjärt* (eng: bright), or the Primordial Mother in the form of Diana/Artemis, torch bearer and goddess of hunt.[3] Here Lucia is regarded a female equivalent or consort of Lucifer–the Lucifera. Her presence is also substantial in the appearance of Virgin Mary who in the hymn *Ave Stella Maris* (eng: Hail, Star of the Sea) brings light to those who are blinded and dwell in darkness; *profer lumen caecis* (en: send forth light to the blind). The numen within the feast of Lucia is also re-

2 In Sweden, Christmas Eve (24th of December) is the main focus of celebration, while Christmas Day (25th of December) is secondary. In 1753 Sweden took the final step in switching over to the Gregorian calendric system from the Julian calendar. During the middle ages, in times of the Julian calendar, the festivities of Lucia, therefore, took place during the winter solstice.

3 Hammarstedt, Edvard af. "Lucia" in *Meddelanden från Nordiska Museet* 1898, P. A. Norstedt & Söner 1900. p19 ff.

markably akin to that of the spirit of Lucifer, the fallen angel of Abrahamic religion, and his appearance in Scandinavian myth. In folklore and Scandinavian Books of Black Arts, Lucifer is often mentioned alongside the other infernal spirits in the process of Satan, and it seems it has also been quite common to regard Lucifer and the Devil as the same principle, or at least he would contribute to a part of the entire infernal image, where Satan is considered as the great Opposer and Adversary. In light of this, there is a betrothed engagement between the Virgin of Light and the Opposer which stretches far beyond mere etymological similarities.

Lucia celebration in Karlstad, Sweden, 1964. Private collection of the Author.

STAFFAN STAR GAZER & DARK LUCIA

While Lucia and Lucifer derive from the Latin word *lux* (en: light) there is also another form of Lucia who is not so much identified with the candle-crowned virgin. One legend states that Lucia is none other than Lilith, the first wife of Adam, who is mentioned in Isaiah 34:14 concerning the vengeance against Edom: *"Wildcats will meet hyenas, the goat demon will call to his friends, and there Lilith will lurk and find her resting place."* In many interpretations, both Lilith/Lucia and Lucifer have been identified with the serpent of Eden, and thus, some rural people in Sweden strongly opposed the festivities surrounding Lucia as it would be regarded a commemoration of the Evil One. In these cases, this dark form of Lucia was directly identified as the Bride of Darkness, sometimes referred to as adulteress, envisioned as a bird of prey scouting for young children to devour; here is a close resemblance with Lilith's relationship to owls and as a murderer of children. One account from the western parts of Sweden states that *"Lucia was believed to be a murderer and in general an evil human. People who wanted to stay reputable therefore never celebrated this feast."*[4]

In Swedish folklore, Lucia can either be a representation of Lilith, or seen coupled with Lucifer. This union should according to myth have created several children which she carried like an animal, and while being devoted only to lust, Lucia is here regarded the mother of supernatural beings and creatures of the night. In Denmark the *ellefolket* (en: forest nymphs, elves) were the descendants of *Lillis* who could *"fly and swim and give birth to several children at a time"*.[5] In some areas, people also regarded Cain as the forefather of supernatural beings in Swedish folklore. When Cain wandered in the land of Nod and found himself a wife, it was with the kin of Lucia he coupled, whose offspring lived at four cubit's depth beneath the ground. This idea can be traced back to at least sometime between the 8th and 11th century CE and the Old English epic poem *Beowulf*, set in Scandinavia, wherein Cain is considered the progenitor of supernatural creatures in general, and foremost of the giant Grendel, the epic's main adversary.

The killing of Abel, all-ruling Father
The kindred of Cain crushed with His vengeance;
In the feud He rejoiced not, but far away drove him
From kindred and kind, that crime to atone for,
Meter of Justice. Thence ill-favored creatures,
Elves and giants, monsters of ocean,
Came into being, and the giants that longtime
Grappled with God; He gave them requital.[6]

4 The Institute for Language and Folklore (Sweden), IFGH 3406 p. 1.

5 Johansson, Levi. "Lucia och de underjordiske i norrländsk folksägen". *Fataburen*, 1906. pp. 193–97.

6 Hall, Leslie (trans.) Beowulf–An Anglo-Saxon Epic Poem, D. C. Heath & Co., Publishers 1892. p. 5.

According to North European legend, Staffan Stalledräng or Sankte Stefan (St Stephen) was stoned to death accused of blasphemy and due to his service as King Herod's stableman he came to be known, among other things, as the patron saint of horses, which is an important folkloristic aspect of his appearance. The same legend states that Staffan saw the Star of Bethlehem shining brightly in the sky and went to Herod to inform that the new king was born. Herod claimed it to be nonsense and said it was just as impossible as if the rooster he had just been served for dinner would rise from the dead. When the rooster did just that, rose from the dead and crowed "Christ is born", Herod had Stephen stoned to death. In the light of this event, Staffan was a stargazer or a man receiving revelation from the stars. Lucifer in the form of the Fallen Morning Star, as we recognize him through his etymological concurrence in Isaiah 14:12 *"How art thou fallen from heaven, O Lucifer, son of the morning!"* can here be considered the angel-beast, with human host, fallen from heaven to the realm of men. Staffan would then be regarded the revelator of the Lucia procession, he who first sees the star, a diviner of the people, for according to Acts 6:15 it is also known *"that his face was like the face of an angel."* While Lucifer is the Morning Star, also known as the planet Venus, it is particularly interesting to note how modern astronomers have theorized around the idea that the Star of Bethlehem was, in fact, an astronomical occurrence where Venus and Jupiter were seen in alignment in the night sky. This would fit well together with a version of the traditional Staffan carol from the eastern parts of Sweden:

> *No day in sight*
> *though it may seem*
> *it is the bright star*
> *who travels before the day.*[7]

St Stephen is commemorated on the 26th of December and like many folk myths it is not always easy to say where heathen customs end and the Christian ones begin. To add to the confusion, there once was a missionary, one of the first Swedish bishops, called Stefinn or Stephanus who may have been woven together with the more internationally known St Stephen. The 26th of December or Boxing Day, was a day auspicious for magical operations for Swedish country folk. Farm workers would get up early in

7 Hammarstedt, pp. 18–19.

the morning to clear out the dung in the barn, and while there was a lot of mischievous trickery connected to this day, it was also a day dedicated to securing the crops and livestock for the coming year. One of the magical tasks was performed with the aid of horses, which is interesting in the light of St Stephen as their patron saint. Rural folk took their horses to a water hole, preferably a stream running towards the north, and allowed the horse to drink, ideally from a bucket in which a silver spoon had been placed. Other methods included drinking from three different streams, and in several places this practice was arranged as a competition. In this way, success was drawn into the farm or carried home, through equestrian feats. The customs during this day also included going from house to house while singing songs[8] in return for gifts and food, which would serve as meals during the intermediate days between Christmas and New Year's Day. This was called the *lussifärd* (en: Lussi Drive), although, this name, in particular, would also denote the roaming of dark creatures and deceased people in the skies, which also connects these events to the European image of the Wild Hunt, led by none other than Odin in his dark guise, wherein it was also the custom to leave some hay for Odin's horse outside the barn. In Norway, the *lussifärd* was led by Lucia herself, called Mistress of the Mountain, in reference to the abode of trolls,[9] and she is seen riding a wagon while carrying a mysterious brew. In Germany, as previously noted, she may also have been linked to Perchta. In the Swedish province of Härjedalen, a pilgrimage route runs along the two mountains Fruhågna and Lussefjäll. The latter is the mountain of Lusse who is considered the original mother of chthonian creatures, while the mountain Fruhågna stands opposite of her and is occupied by the Virgin Mary. Here, the aspect of Lusse is more that of a spirit or goddess related to Lilith or Lucifer than the saint of Syracuse we originally connected her with.

One of the most commonly known carols called Staffan Stalledräng, still sung today, describes Staffan in relation to the star.

Staffan was a stableboy
And we are very grateful
He gave his five colts water
All to the great star

8 During mid 18th Century the Swedish hymn *"Light of Light, o morningstar"* was common during the end of the term in public schools of southern Sweden.

9 Lusse/Lussi has also been considered to be a troll, living under a bridge.

No day in sight
The stars upon the sky they shine and sparkle

The carol also includes another verse in which one line reads: *"before the crow of the rooster [...] Staffan went to the stable"* which can both be a reference to the early morning activities undertaken on the 13th and also the crowing of Herod's resurrected rooster. The rooster was a guardian on the threshold, and as he would crow at the break of dawn, light would again shine into the world of the living.[10] In the Swedish Black Book *Salomonic Magical Arts* several spells incorporate the use of cock's blood to write out obscure 'Wittenberg letters' for gaining wisdom or riches, or punishing thieves. The blood of a white cock is also said to make horses agile if put on the horse shoe. In the same Black Book we also find a spell calling upon Lucifer to make a horse limp. This does not imply that Lucifer had any spell casting connections with horses in the tradition, however, we are moving about in occult matters related to horse magic, and the rooster was particularly important for esoteric practice in relation to the infernal hierarchy.

As is known, Lucia Night (between 12th & 13th of December) was considered the longest night of the year, a time when the horses were said to be able to talk, when dark forces moved about the countryside and it was generally beneficial to gain contact with the deceased. But Lucia Night was also a time for festivities, celebrating the end of the farming chores before Christmas. All work was prohibited and in particular spinning motions, wherefore all activities related to the mills and grinding were evaded. At this time, the Mill of the World (Grotte) would stand still, the sun would cease its motion and the gates to the underworld stood wide open.[11] Herein is a controversial theory regarding the etymology of the word Christmas, called *jul* in Swedish. The words *jul* (eng: Christmas) and *hjul* (eng: wheel) is pronounced in the same way, which is why the holiday was by some believed to have gained its name related to these events. It is also worth to consider the notion of the unlucky number 13 as a number related to disaster and misfortune. However, there are many stories of how the mills were the targets of sabotage by Lussi, a supernatural curse that could be reversed by throwing fire into the mill-wheel. This was also a night particularly beneficial for the *årsgång* and other magical operations pertaining to the nightside. Årsgång is described as a divinatory method

10 In some areas it was also believed that the rooster was pacified during Lucia night.

11 Hammarstedt 1900:8.

for the coming year, during which the operator should remain alone in a dark room in abstinence, without food and drink. Around midnight he or she would visit the nearest church (or the crossroads), circumambulate it three times counter-clockwise to expel all Christian influences, and blow in the keyhole of the church door every time it was passed. This culminated in different challenges from the spirit world, and if they were overcome, the operator was allowed to gaze into the future. It was also believed that around this day or the coming days before Christmas, Lussi was seen roaming the countryside, sometimes as a woman dressed in white with a baker's peel in both hands, scouting for children to abduct, particularly Christian children.

This is Lucifer in the form of the Morning Star, consort of Lucia/Lilith, a truly celestial being radiating from a mythical firmament above. We now turn to Lucifer in the form of Adversary, Opposer or Devil. In this form he is more material, the Devil who walks the earth, with whom the humans may sign pacts or even witness with their own physical eyes. There is a great body of legends and stories related to Lucifer in this form, but we will focus on the auspicious time around Christmas.

LUCIFER'S KIN

The above mentioned Lucia buns are a popular ingredient in a successful Lucia celebration. They are made from simple wheat dough, flavored with precious saffron, and like many prevalent folk customs it is believed to have derived from Germany, probably sometime during the 17th century. The common name for these buns in Sweden is directly translated *Lucia Cats*, or more specifically *Lusse Cats* or *Lussi Cats* (swe: lussekatter, lussikatter) while it is customary in many areas to bake the buns into representing the faces of cats.[12] It is widely believed that the nocturnal cat animal is a form of dark spirit and even more so, the black cat, which was believed to be a familiar spirit of the Devil. Cats should, according to custom, be treated with care and respect. It was strictly forbidden to kill a cat, and any rifle that had failed to follow this rule was forever useless. However, the only way permitted by which one could take the life of a cat was through drowning, as the

12 It is, however, uncertain how old this custom is. Today, in general, the Lucia bun is baked into the shape of an S.

animal was connected to the *Neck* and the water nymphs–the kindred of Lucifer. The Neck has even been called by his alternative name–River Cat.

One theory says that these buns derive from Germany where St Nicholaus, the predecessor of the modern Santa Claus, handed out cookies for the children. At some point, the buns got their name *dövelskatter* or *dyvelskatter*–Devil's Cats. In for example Germany, France, and the Netherlands, St Nicholaus is accompanied by a black man during his Christmas procession through the city. This figure is known as Black Pete and has the function of a sacred clown, a mischievous character who also hands out candy, but his function can also be similar to that of Krampus, the horned Alpine beast-man who torments the naughty children and hands out boons to the obedient. This role is also reserved for the Bavarian Nussmärtel, a pack of black men in long beards who carry away ill-behaved children in their sacks. These figures are all representations of the Opposer of the light; wild and threatening, who work their ways outside the governed customs of civilized society. As forces of misrule which are both accusing and demanding, they encourage people to take responsibility for their own actions, hearkening back to the ancient temptation and promise of the serpent. Thus, in Perchta-Krampus we can see similar elements as in the Scandinavian Lucia-Lucifer/Devil. It may sound harsh to couple Lucia, the pious Christian saint, with Lucifer or the Devil; however, it is important to understand that the folk belief often transgressed the ideas of dogma and morale; in the minds of the common people it was thus possible to acknowledge both virgin and harlot in the same personification. There is a Swedish saying that goes: *"Where God will build a church, the Devil will soon build a chapel."* This expression carries multiple meanings, the most obvious being that, on earth, the Devil imitates God, while the Devil is also always on the watch, observing every step humanity takes. Contrary to the belief that the Devil would despise dwelling in the church and around consecrated areas, there are several accounts of how the Devil appears in church, for it was a place beneficial for supernatural powers and magical operations in general.

There is a concept, more or less widespread in the body of Swedish folklore, that the Luciferian Fall originated several nocturnal deities on earth. In some cases, the genesis of these spirits is marked by the fall imagined in relation to places of power and a mythic interpretation of the origin of nature spirits and the spirits of the place.

She believed that Lucifer's company had fallen from heaven down to earth, where some had settled in the water and are now called water sprites,13 beneath houses that are called brownies, beneath the trees as elves, in the forests as forest nymphs or sirens of the woods.[14]

This short narrative comes in many similar forms, in some cases the major force of evil that was cast out was Satan instead of Lucifer, while Satan was said to be able to take the shape of a red dragon roaming the skies. While Lucifer and his loyal angels were thrown down into the deepest pits of hell, the lesser evil spirits and angels roamed the earth and recognized each other with their moaning voices. The brownie was, for example, an important spirit, who contrary to modern depictions as a cute, compliant short man, was a rather harsh and aggressive figure, crucial for the longevity of the farm, who had to be appeased in order continue his benevolent duties. There are even accounts of how country folks sacrificed food to the brownie upon a birch altar during Lucia Night, where something was presented to him from each and every one of the guests.[15]

The Swedish word *vittra* as a general term for supernatural beings has also been referred to as *Lucia's kin*. Once Lucifer had been thrown down from heaven he tried to climb back up upon a branch of the brier. When God noticed his attempt, he quickly turned the thorns so that they pointed downwards, ensuring that Lucifer remained fallen. Humans were not totally distinguished from the *vittra* or other creatures of Lucifer's race, for all humans possessed a fetch or phantom which would walk the underworld in the same manner as the physical body walked above ground *"following her as the shadow followed the body."*[16] The underground shape and its human host were attached at the feet, and it was possible to catch a glimpse of one's fetch when gazing into the mirror image produced by a lake, or similar natural water surface. The fetch and the human were tightly bound together and anything that befell one of them was also transferred to the other, both in terms of magical diseases related to the primal elements, and the interaction with creatures of Lucifer's kin. While these chthonic

13 Näcken.

14 Linné 1745:312. Other versions also include the idea that the spirits who fell upon the mountains became trolls.

15 The Institute for Language and Folklore (Sweden), VFF 1781 p. 1.

16 Linné, Carl von. *Öländska och Gothländska Resa*. Stockholm och Upsala hos Gottfried Kiesewetter, 1745. pp. 312–13.

creatures were considered offspring of Lucifer/Lilith, the elves were in some cases the offspring of Eve. One Icelandic story says that when Eve was preparing to present her children before God she didn't have time to tend to all of them and thus she hid them in shame, before the face of God. God approached Eve and asked to see all of her children, and as a result of her untidiness, God said: *"What has been kept hidden from me will be kept hidden from the humans."* Thus were the *hidden people* created, or the elves, which were also children of Eve, but remained concealed in contrast to the humans who were presented before God.

The common concept of Lucifer in Sweden seems to have been that of Lord of Darkness, the fallen angel, he who is both Devil and Satan. Many names have been used for the ultimate evil in Swedish folklore: *Djävulen* (eng: the Devil), Satan, Lucifer, Lussi, Skam, Fan, Hin Onde, Hin Håle, Nyger or in relation to Lucia he could even be Lusse-Pär or *Lussegubben* (eng: Lusse Man).[17] The ultimate evil is also quite commonly found in the complexity of Odin, and there are examples where he has taken the role of similar powers across Europe, as seen in for example the Wild Hunt. In the Swedish Black Book tradition Lucifer is called alongside infernal spirits, such as Beelzebub and Asmodeus, while the Satanic pact or congress with the Devil was a method of gaining supernatural powers and protection. Priests who had the benefit of attending the notorious School of Wittenberg, where the Black Arts were studied, had the opportunity to study in depth the *6th and 7th Book of Moses*; a person who had that sort of information was surely able to command the powers of the Devil. While humans were an easy prey for the forces of darkness, as taught by the Lutheran church, so was it also possible to act according to a more personal will, or the will of the community by the means and methods of magic. The hidden people and the elves that were once hidden from God by Eve, the offspring of Cain and the chthonic creatures of Lucifer's race were accessible to the knowledgeable man.

17 Lussegubben has also been regarded the same creature as Will-o'-the-wisp, i.e. one of Lucifer's kin. He would rule the darkest night and could be seen out in the night sowing seeds in the field. In some parts of Sweden, men would dress up as Lussegubben, in yet another form, and roam the Lucia night with mischief and trickery.

THE PACT AND THE BOOK

With Lucifer's Fall and the banishment from Eden, the eyes of humanity were opened, the same eyes gouged from the sockets of St Lucy of Syracuse, and mankind gained knowledge of good and evil and defined morale precious to the governing of society and the progression of the human species. The eyesight was not lost, but upon death restored and improved, for the new eyes of men were of a divine and nocturnal origin. These new eyes could be used to see the hidden people, creatures of the night and those of Lucifer's and Lucia's race, and thus man gained the knowledge of magic, and the uses of right and wrong. The magician or cunning person putting the Book of Black Arts into service possessed great powers for he or she had the knowledge to conjure with force the devils and fallen angels from Hell and back again. This was often made possible by the aid of the divine powers through the Holy Trinity or *Pater Noster* (eng: Our Father) as a protective means against the infernal powers one would want to put into service. But conjure, sorcery and other more modest acts of magic or cunning were only possible because of the *pacta cum Diabolo*–Pact with the Devil, which juridically was labelled as *crimen laesae majestatis Divinae*–crime against the crown of God. Some beliefs reckon the celebration of Lucia as the worship of Lucifer, which was not a far-fetched assumption for a Lutheran, as Luther said that the Devil was a master of disguise and that he would trick humans by shifting shape. Luther even stated that "*he dresses as if he was God himself*"[18] and it was also a common belief that the Devil would walk among the people, hence the expression '*folk eller fan?*' (eng: man or Devil?).[19]

While humanity was, in Christian terms, regarded as the crown of creation, Lucifer and his company were doomed to walk the earth until Judgment Day, when they would turn into human form. It was also believed that Lucifer had a sort of longing to become human, or at least he shared a great interest in human existence. In this reality, the fallen angels and the humans were closely linked together by a kinship not only dependent on the Original Sin, but as a result thereof. The complexity lies within the great variation of local belief and practice, while it is difficult to give a uni-

18 Wolf-Knuts, Ulrika. *Människan och djävulen–En studie kring form, motiv och funktion I folklig tradition*. Åbo akademis förlag 1991, p. 139.
19 Ibid., p. 138.

fied picture of the relationship with the infernal spirits. The offspring of Eve resulted in humanity, while Lilith, as the first wife of Adam, was the mother of supernatural beings, creatures in Swedish folklore that inhabited nature–Lucifer's kin. We may also note that Eve was the first human to commit a sin for which humanity was banished from Eden, and later found their settlement in Nod, Edom or Sodom and Gomorra. Two of the deadliest sins were pride and bravado according to the devotional texts of the Lutheran church, and it is known that Lucifer fell due to arrogance or pride. But the folklore also gives the alternative version that God was not able to control Lucifer, which was the reason for the fall.

The pact with the Devil was in Sweden and Scandinavia either performed by a written contract or other more or less common ritual procedures, such as renouncing the name of God, while *magia daemoniaca* or *magia illicita* encompassed all magical practices in the Devil's name. The Norwegian manuscript known as the *Black Books of Elverum* inaugurates the gathering of spells with three quite extensive workings dedicated to Lucifer and the infernal spirits. The reader is told how to release the angels of hell, renounce God, "to conjure up the evil spirits" and how to control them. Lucifer is here called upon as the Ruler of the Dark Abyss, and one should enter into complete dedication to the fallen angel if releasing the angels of hell:

> *"The day you will release and follow after Lucifer, you should rise in the Devil's name, get dressed in the Devil's name. Yes! Wash, comb your hair, and go out in the Devil's name. Everything that you undertake shall happen in the Devil's name that day."*[20]

In the Norwegian Black Book tradition as well as in the Swedish, both Lucifer and Belzebub are common agents to hire for service in matters of catching thieves or bashing the eyes out of a thief, binding spells, or in workings related to offensive or protective magic. Despite the type of practitioner—whether a servant of Christ and Lord God, or of Lucifer, Lord of Darkness—the following excerpt from a binding prayer, from southern Sweden, demonstrates the connection between Lucifer and supernatural creatures of the night.

20 Rustad, p. 7

Kyrie eleison! Lord God, father in the heavens, have mercy on the servant of Jesus Christ N. N.; kyrié eleison, Christ, have mercy on this servant of Jesus Christ N. N., Lord God, Holy Spirit have mercy over this servant of Jesus Christ, so that you Devil will–by the † of God Father, by the † of the Son of God, by the † of God the Holy Spirit–turn away all evil caused to this man, inside or outside house.

Are you of the ten compartments of Hell, or are you submitted to the same, or are you of the uttermost Proses, or the first in Hell, or the servant of Lucifer, or are you north-flying, west-flying, south-flying or east-flying, or are you Roncres or fearless, above earth, or below earth, or are you the Ring Devil, who is called troll-folk, with the Devil by your side, as he has God on his, who pushed the devil Lucifer, Belsebub, with his evil and vicious company down from the heaven wherein God lives; in the same way the same God who commands the above mentioned devils, shall not do harm to his cattle or anything else.

Are you evil humans, are you elves, are you the vattenhästen[21] *are you gårpyker, are you forest nymph, are you mountain troll, are you hysemoder, are you in system or under the table, are you a ghost, are you adergång, are you geroglon, are you vester, are you belsevättar, are you earth-bugan, or other upsyke, or what evil can it be?*[22]

Lucia and Staffan, Lilith and Lucifer stand as pillars in vigil on both sides of Christmas, the darkest and most dangerous time of the year, but also one of the most magically potent times when a crack opens up between our world and the spirit world, and communication with spirits of Lucifer's kin is possible. Lucia/Lilith is the bringer of light for those who dwell in darkness, she comes with light in the darkest of times, and like Prometheus she brings the fire into the hearts of men and bestows knowledge upon them. Coupled with Lucifer/Devil we see a pair of culture heroes, discoverers of forbidden knowledge, the black arts, the art of divination, and, as the first wife of Adam, Lucia/Lilith is the progenitor of earth's supernatural be-

21 Vattenhäst (eng: Water Horse) or the more common *bäckahäst* (eng: River Horse) is the Neck, the water spirit, in the form of a horse. What follows is a list of several corrupted names of nature spirits and dark creatures related to Lucifer's kin.

22 Wigström, Eva. *Folkdiktning, visor, folktro, sägner och en svartkonstbok.* Torsten Hedlunds Förlag, 1881, pp. 382.

ings. The gouged eyes of Lucia and the plucked eye of Odin serve as myths of affliction in a complex image connecting different aspects of the Wild Hunt and the roaming of dark spirits, a nexus of the deceased— one eye on the plate and one in the well of knowledge, both served as a self-sacrifice. When we speak of Lussi in Swedish folklore, the image can range from the leader of the Wild Hunt to St Lucy of Syracuse, from Lilith to Lucifer. Whosoever sees the Fallen Angel or the Woman in White will be greeted by the Devil–*profer lumen caecis*!

Lucifer in La Ville-Lumière

Madeleine LeDespencer

PARIS AT THE turn of the 19th century was a glittering epicenter of art, culture, and commerce. As the heart of both commercial and bohemian Europe, the city burned brightly enough to earn the enduring honorific 'La Ville-Lumière' or City of Light. Beneath the veneer of this continental metropolis could be found another Paris, fed by the murky tributaries of la Bièvre, the Seine's lost sister river; long disappeared beneath the streets of the city. This demimonde was populated by alchemists, Satanists, degenerates, and mystics and reigning over this marvelous secret Paris, was a single spirit of the zeitgeist, the shining star of Lucifer.

The culture of the late 19th century moved with a velocity never before seen. Stoked by the fires of the industrial revolution, change was omnipresent. The same engines of transformation that were forever altering the countrysides and cities were also irreversibly reshaping the face of European culture. In the preceding century, monarchs had fallen in elaborate blood sacrifice to birth a new republic and old orders were cast aside. At the end of the 19th century the once powerful church of Rome found itself in decline and the hitherto accepted social strata seemed to erode beneath the feet of the traditionalists. Social progress was making its first strides in the movement for workers rights, and rights for women. The air was alight with liberty.

As with any culture in transition, a variety of new religious movements sprung up in the wake of this shifting order. The age of reason gave way to a revival of the esoteric. Much like the mystery cults of Late Antiquity, as one order fell away it opened cracks in the facade of civilization through which flickered a primordial divine. Among the occultists of Paris a re-emergence of an ancient theme could be found. A resurgence of a gnostic tradition pressed between naked flesh, in sabbath fires, and on the lips of renegade priests.

It was in this environment that a Luciferian-Satanic gnosis resurged in the popular consciousness. The fallen angel had already been a favourite inspiration for the authors of the previous century, and the romantic reading of Lucifer would find fertile ground in the decadent imagination. Luciferian power was readily apparent all around with the rapid industrialization of the cities of Europe, the transformation of social order, the upsetting of sexual norms, and all manifestations of such Uranian energies. The spirit of the abjected angel, the liberator and morning star (Lucifer in the feminine aspect, Venus) saturated every aspect of Parisian life from high art and culture to the hidden chambers of the fringe occultists.

Theologically speaking, Satan and Lucifer are not one but rather two distinct personas. Lucifer is the rebel angel, the most beautiful of the heavenly host often identified with Sabaoth, and the morning star—Venus. Satan, on the other hand, is not an individual but a role or office. He is an accuser or contrarian. Satan is the tempter while Lucifer is the liberator. These rather pronounced differences were generally disregarded by the Romantic movement who took Satan/Lucifer as a symbol of rebellion and liberation. From Milton to Shelly and then later with Baudelaire, Satan often played a dual role of spoiler and liberator.

In some cases, the distinction between Satan and Lucifer became an object of poetic license, an esoteric illustration of transformation. This was the case with Victor Hugo and his Manichaean poem, *La Fin de Satan*. Hugo believed that when humanity's vision was clarified, evil disappeared. Evil, to Hugo, was merely an emptiness filled with the futility of ill deeds, a void he called "Satan." Once illuminated this entity transforms in an inferno of freedom, along with all of mankind, into a liberating Lucifer. To Hugo, Satan was merely an unrealized, lesser emanation of Lucifer as evidenced in the line:

"Satan is no more, be born again, O celestial Lucifer!"

At this unprecedented time, all the world was in revolution but there seemed to be one constant to which the artists, writers, and esotericists all held. Something greater was coming, and it would transform us all, forever.

THE AGE OF THE PARACLETE

The occult milieu of 19th century Paris, unlike its Anglophone counterpart, was steeped in an occult Catholicism with deep roots set in pre-Christian gnostic sources. Martinism and Freemasonry laid the primary foundation of the French occult revival suffused with intimations of gnostic heresies. Among many of the most prominent esotericists of the era, there was a common thread, borrowed from esoteric Christianity, the Coming Age of the Paraclete.

The Paraclete is the third portion of the trinitarian formula, the Holy Ghost. It is most often depicted as a descending Dove, as seen on the Lamen of the Ordo Templi Orientis and previous to that in an illustration accompanying Sar Péladan's *L'Art Idéaliste & Mystique: Doctrine de L'Ordre et du Salon Annuel des Rose+Croix.* We must note that the Paraclete, as the holy spirit, is most often identified with the feminine aspect of the trinity.

It is also tied intrinsically to the history of France and the mysteries of divine Kingship. Every King of France since Clovis was anointed with an oil said to be brought to Earth by the Paraclete and no man attains kingship without being immersed in the power of the feminine aspect.

The coming of the Paraclete is an age-old theory first put forth by Joachim of Flora in his *Theory of Three Ages.* The doctrine of the Paraclete held that mankind was in an ongoing transformation manifested by the successive unveiling of the trinity. In the first age, that of the Old Testament, God had been revealed to humanity. In the subsequent age of the Sun, Yeshua comes upon the world. It is this final coming age of the Holy Ghost that so interested the occultists and mystics. This third and final term of the trinity was the coming Paraclete that would descend on a transformed humanity and help them transcend original sin and the limitations of the flesh. In their heretical reading, the function of the Holy Ghost is an explicitly sexual nature. As Huysmans says in the novel *La Bas*, while describing the doctrine of heretical priests Eugene Vintras and Abbé Boullan (about whom we shall read more in due course):

> *The action of the Paraclete... extends to the generative principle the divine life sanctifies organs which henceforth can procreate only those who are elect, beings exempt from original sin, beings it will not be necessary to test in the fires of pain and suffering.*

The Paraclete is directly tied to the sexual principal. To be ready for this age of the Paraclete the congregations needed to have transcended original sin and have become cleansed by sexual unions in the name of spiritual reparation. The notion could not be any more Luciferian, freedom from the chains of restriction and enlightenment in the exploration of love and flesh. Regarding the Luciferian aspect of the Paraclete, Eliphas Levi himself said in *The Mysteries of Magic:*

> *What is more absurd and more impious than to attribute the name of Lucifer to the devil, that is, to personified evil. The intellectual Lucifer is the spirit of intelligence and love; it is the Paraclete, it is the Holy Spirit, while the physical Lucifer is the great agent of universal magnetism.*

The three most influential proponents of this coming age were the trinity of Eugene Vintras, Joseph-Antoine Boullan and Maria de Naglowaska. All three were mystics who recognized the primary role of women in their new church and sought gnosis via a sacred sexuality that bridged opposites, dwelled in the forbidden, and sought transcendence via transgression. Boulan and Vintras were both joined by shadow visionary women who served as spiritual guides and partners while Naglowaska was her own iconoclastic self-styled 'Satanic Woman' who sought to create a new religion guided by a sisterhood of sexual initiatrixes bringing her new sensual religion to the world.

The erotic Paracleteism of these three centered on transcendence via carnality. This doctrine has been called 'ascensional redemption' or as Stanislas de Guaita named it; "the great Arcanum of the Carmel." In this process the body is used as a vehicle of attainment to undo original sin by indulging in extremes of sensation. By engaging with the Virgin Mary and her mediatrixes of spirit, sexuality becomes the greatest sacrament by which the original prelapsarian state of the soul could be restored. This is the Reparation of Boullan or the Reintegration of the Martinists. The aim is the same even if the path differs. Ostensibly Christian on the surface, this Luciferianism is rooted in sources far older and speaks to survivals of pre Christian mystery cults of eroto-ecstatic attainment and ritualized inversion.

L'ABBÉ BOULLAN

Joseph-Antoine Boullan was born January 18, 1824, in Saint-Porquier. He studied for the priesthood in Rome where he graduated with distinction. After serving for a time with The Missionaries of the Precious Blood, he moved to Paris as an independent priest. It was here that he published his first book in 1853, a translation of the Spanish nun Maria d'Agreda's *la Vie Divine de la Sainte Vierge*, a visionary retelling of the life of the Virgin Mary. In Paris, Boullan was chosen to serve as the spiritual guide to Adèle Chevalier, a young Belgian nun from the convent Saint-Thomas-de-Villeneuve in Soissons. Adèle was experiencing visionary trance and Marian apparitions and Boullan became her companion.

Together Adèle and Boullan formed a religious community called The Society for the Reparation of Souls and by all accounts, the two became lovers. The goal of the society was Reintegration of the human soul by restoring it to an Edenic state. Together, they published an anonymous manifesto under the title *La Veritable Reparation Ou L'Ame Reparatrice Par Les Saintes Larmes de Jesus Et de Marie.*

The pair were said to heal afflictions of the body and soul 'by strange means.' Rumours swirled about the pair suggesting they were engaging in sexual rites and other transgressions with the congregation. Boullan never shied away from the breaking of taboos in his spirituality, in fact, it appeared to be a core aspect of his doctrine. His method of spiritual healing reads heavily with intimations of the inversion practices of gnostic sects such as the Borborites, incorporating as it were mixtures of communion wafers, blood, and feces. It was said he exorcized the afflicted by spitting in mouths and having parishioners drink their own urine mixed with that of Adèle.

Among the most sacred rites of the group were two specific operations; *Unions of Wisdom* and *Unions of Charity*. Both were essentially sexual rites. The *Union of Wisdom* involved participants engaging in sexual congress with higher spiritual beings, saints, and some chosen humans while the *Union of Charity* involved sexual congress with ordinary humans and lesser elemental spirits. The idea being that these sexual rites might assist a lower being in its quest toward reparation.

The situation came to a head with allegations that Adèle had conceived a child with Boullan which the two had sacrificed in one of their ceremonies. In 1861 the pair were recalled to Rome and tried for indecency and fraud. Boullan served 3 years for fraud and was forced to write a confession of his crimes. This notebook came to be known as *La Cahir Rose* and to this day is stored in the Vatican archives.

In the winter of 1869, Boullan was considered rehabilitated and returned to Paris. Immediately upon his return he began to publish a new journal, *les Annales de la Sainteté au XIXe siècle.* The journal was so full of heresies it brought him again to the attention of the ecclesiastical authorities. As a result of his continued transgressions Boullan was placed under interdict and as a result he requested to be laicized and so left the Roman Catholic church.

It was at this time Boullan made contact with Pierre Eugene Michel Vintras, the notorious prophet of Tilly-sur-Seulles. Vintras founded his mission on a vision in which the Archangel Michael, Mary, and St Joseph appeared to him to announce the coming age of the Paraclete. Vintras declared himself the reincarnation of the biblical prophet Elijah and founded his order *Oeuvre de Miséricorde* (Work of Mercy). He traveled the countryside performing miracles such as levitation and the production of bleeding hosts all the while building a following of lay people and priests.

LEFT: *Julie Thibault in her youth. Courtesy Bibliothèque de l'Arsenal, Paris.*

Vintras and Boullan met twice in 1875 and, upon the death of Vintras, Boullan declared himself the successor of the prophet and the reincarnation of John the Baptist. A portion of Vintras congregation decided to follow Boullan and they established a church at Lyon. Among the members was Mme Julie Thibault, the woman who would take Adèle's place by Boullan's side as Magdalene, medium, and partner.

Thibault began her spiritual journey at the age of 17 when she left her husband and set out on foot to visit every Marian shrine in France. The 19th Century is known in Catholic circles as 'The Age of Mary', this 100 year period featured an unusual and vibrant clustering of Marian apparitions around the world. These manifestations seemed to correspond with a general resurfacing of the feminine aspect in the spirituality of the West.

This return of the feminine can be classified as a particularly Luciferian eruption. Lucifer has been long connected with the spirit of liberation, especially with regards to women and the Edenic narrative. It was the Serpent Samael in the garden who first showed Eve the path to be 'as God.' If the perfected, natural state of spirit is an androgynous being, the first step to become 'as God' is to reconcile and reclaim the feminine which has been systematically denigrated by a debased spirituality.

This ingress of Lucifer's fire manifested in the feverish visions of mystics like Julie Thibault who were, by their nature, liminal beings. It was an influx which would not be contained and manifested in inspired heresies. In 1888 Jules Doinel, librarian, Freemason, and Spiritist began to experience communications from what he deemed to be 'the Divine Feminine Aspect.' He took from these visions his life mission to restore the sacred feminine to religion, to rebuild the church of the Sophia, and to revive the work of the Cathars and their predecessors. As a result of these communications, Doniel would found the Eglise Gnostique Universelle Catholique, establishing one of the enduring lines of Gnostic bishops still extant to this day.

In response to these Marian apparitions, Julie lived on nothing but bread, milk and honey and walked nearly 30,000 miles on her mission. Devoutly committed to the Virgin she considered herself "a priestess of Mary." She was particularly drawn to the shrine at La Salette and its apocalyptic message which she considered "the virgin for the few" as opposed to Lourdes "the virgin of the many.' She came to the congregation of Vintras in 1874 and by 1883 was a full member of Boullan's congregation in Lyon where she took full participation in the central rites Sacrifice of the Glory of Melchizedek and the Provictimal Sacrifice of Mary.

Thibault was a striking woman, dressed always in black with a prayer book in hand and a small crucifix around her neck. She would be known by various appellations in the congregation including Achildael, *l'Espouse Josephique*, and most interestingly *La Femme Apostolique* 'The Apostolic Woman.' The latter implies a female priesthood with full agency, a notion wholly at odds with the church of Rome but well keeping with the traditions of some Gnostic heresies. Boullan, like Maria de Naglowska after him, would recognize and implement the integral role of the sacred feminine in the role of religious reintegration.

Following the death of Boullan, Mme Thibault would move into Huysmans' flat on rue de Sèvres as lodger and housekeeper. Here, she would continue to perform the Provictimal Sacrifice of Mary daily, using a small tabernacle she brought from Lyon for this very purpose. Donning green and white vestments, Mme Thibault would enact the mass in Huysmans' apartments.

Huysmans would explain some aspects Boullan's rites in his novel *La Bas*. In chapter 20 we are treated to a lengthy discussion of the theories of Vintras and Dr. Johannes, a character based largely on Boullan. In the chapter the astrologer Gévingey explains the import of Sacrifice of the Glory of Melchizedek as such.

> *Theology teaches us that the mass, as it is celebrated, is the re-enaction of the Sacrifice of Calvary, but the sacrifice to the glory of Melchizedek is not that. It is, in some sort, the future mass, the glorious office which will be known during the earthly reign of the divine Paraclete. This sacrifice is offered to God by man regenerated, redeemed by the infusion of the Love of the Holy Ghost.*

To Vintras, the ecclesiastical mass represents the supreme sacrifice of the current age, the age of the Son while The Sacrifice of the Glory of Melchizedek is a mass of the future offered by regenerated men and women infused with the power of pure love. This love is described by Boullan's biographer Joanny Bricaud as the aforementioned sexual Unions of Wisdom and Unions of Charity.

To truly grasp this concept of union we need to understand how Boullan understood the fall of man and the Luciferian role in that narrative. Boullan believed that the fall was triggered by human sexuality becoming reduced to base carnality and therefore divorced from its higher purpose. This state was brought about in the garden of Eden as a byproduct of a sexual union between the first couple and the beings Lilith and Samael.

According to Rabbinical writings, Samael and Lilith are unable to achieve sexual union of their own accord, but instead require the use of an intermediary to mate. In the garden, Lilith and Samael conjoined to form the adversarial serpent that liberates Eve. The pair, in a hermaphroditic form, used Adam and Eve as a bridge to facilitate their joining. The first sexual act of humanity was not between two humans, but with an androgynous spirit. This resulted not only in the wisdom to be 'as god' but also in the birth of a host of lesser spirits or demons.

Altar used by Boullan and Julie Thibault, with a copy of the Provictimal Sacrifice of Mary. Courtesy Bibliothèque de l'Arsenal, Paris.

The wisdom to which Adam and Eve were awakened was to their own carnal nature and to the divisions between their bodies. It allowed them the power of reproduction, sexual union, and the exercise of their free will but it also divorced them from a more perfect spiritual sexual union. It is this fractured state that Boullan sought to reconcile with his 'work of mercy.' Even those lesser spirits born from the union of Lilith/Samael might be helped to reconciliation via the aforementioned Unions of Charity. To Boullan, it was only by the mystical application of sexuality that the spirit could be saved. As he wrote in his journal:

> *humanity is degraded by a double adultery, in the persons of Adam, stained with the caresses Lilith and Eve who is withered by the kiss of Samael: the body and vitality of the first couple were infected at their source...*

The whole of Boullan's work was an attempt to rectify this spiritual damage and liberate humanity by the sexuality they had so feared and abused. It was a noble and tender endeavour born of love. Joanny Bricaud wrote eloquently how Boullan sought to repair this aspect of humanity with his life's work:

> *Since the Fall from grace resulted from an illicit act of love, the Redemption of Humanity can only be achieved through acts of love accomplished in a religious manner...guilty love must be combated through pure love, through a sexual approach, but in a heavenly manner, to the spirits in order to raise oneself: this is the union of wisdom.*

Boullan passed away on January 4, 1893, in Lyon. Huysmans and many of his close circle were convinced it was a result of a magical battle with Stanislas de Guaita with whom he had been feuding for some time. The priest's papers were left with Huysmans and the Church of Carmel passed on to Pascal Misme. The Boullanian and Vintrasian lineage of consecrations continue to this day within various gnostic churches.

MARIA DE NAGLOWSKA

Where Vintras and Boullan celebrated the role of the feminine in the spirituality of the Paraclete and both worked closely with oracular women, it was not until the 1930s that a woman would emerge as her own advocate and evangelist, spreading a doctrine of Luciferian love and enlightened sexuality. Her name was Maria de Naglowska. Known to her students as *the Satanic Woman* or *Sophia of Montparnasse*, Maria's vision for the future was a new matriarchal religion in which 'heroic men' were instructed in occult knowledge by an initiated sisterhood known as Sophiales. Esoteric wisdom was passed on via sexual unions and humanity would be transformed by the dawning of the feminine aspect of the Trinity, the Holy Ghost.

Maria de Naglowska was born in St Petersburg, Russia in 1883 into a wealthy Czarist family. She was provided with the best education available at the time. She was trained in multiple languages, pedagogy, and philosophy. There are legends that she may have met Rasputin as a child but these remain only as speculation. While growing up among the Carpathian mountains she undoubtedly heard the stories circulating of the notorious fringe religious sect operating at the time in Russia, the Khlysty.

The Khlysty were an offshoot of the Russian Orthodox church who lived in communities called Arks and lead by male and female heads titled Christ and Mother of God, respectively. It was said the order believed that salvation was only attainable by total repentance and to facilitate total repentance one must transgress enthusiastically. According to C. L. Sulzberger, their doctrine encouraged members to "Sin in order that you may obtain forgiveness." Rasputin was accused of being a member of the sect but Sulzberger suggested that he had adopted the philosophy of the group, if not taken full membership.

The premise of the cult is that all men have the potential to be God and all women to be the Virgin. This is attained through the transfiguring descent of the Holy Ghost in sadomasochistic rites of flagellation and dance. The participants would dance in a circle whipping one another into a frenzy until overtaken with this transcendental state in which their sin transforms into a sacrament. Julius Evola theorized the source of these rites was quite ancient and the cult was actually preserving pre-Christian orgiastic rites in a 'degraded form.'

Beyond these influences of her youth, Maria was a Theosophist and there is evidence that she may have been a Co-Mason and was influenced by the work of Eliphas Levi. One must wonder if, in her time in Paris, she did not encounter the remaining followers of Vintras who were very much still active in esoteric circles. Where Vintras and Boullan began with their elaboration on the age of the Paraclete as a sexual mystery Maria further developed it onto a mystical union of flesh, instinct, and direct experience. Her work carries a touch of spiritualist oracular trance that was likely inherited from the influence of The Hermetic Brotherhood of Luxor and P. B. Randolph.

Maria married young to a Jewish musician and Zionist named Moise Hopenko. The couple left Russia and lived in Germany and Switzerland for a time. Her husband then decided to answer his call to Palestine leaving Maria with the children alone. To make ends meet she found work as a journalist and textbook author. As an exceptional linguist and translator, this would serve to be her primary means of income for the rest of her life.

She spent the majority of the 1920s in Rome where she met pagan traditionalist Julius Evola. There she worked as a translator and journalist. She rendered the poetry of Evola into French and he, in turn, translated her work into Italian. Maria would also contribute regularly to the journal *L'Italia*. It was during this time in Rome that Maria experienced her most important initiation.

One day, while en route to the Pius XI papal conclave, Maria encountered an elderly Catholic monk on the street. She would describe this encounter in her newspaper *La Fleche* in 1932, referring to the old monk as "My Spiritual Chief" (terminology reminiscent of Blavatsky and the Golden Dawn). She cited him as the primary source for the doctrine she would promulgate as her life's work.

Maria described how the old monk appeared before her barefoot and hatless. He was dressed in sackcloth with a plain rope tied round his waist. He handed her a piece of cardboard on which was traced a triangle illustrating the trinity. The first two apexes were labeled as Father and Son while the third was indistinct and represented the feminine Holy Ghost. Her mission would be to herald this coming age of this Third Term of the Trinity.

To Maria, the third term of the trinity, the Holy Ghost, was female. The Father heralded Judaism and reason, the Son was the harbinger of Christianity and the heart. The Holy Ghost, on the other hand, represented the feminine and the reconciliation of the forces of light and darkness. Maria would embrace this reconciliation of opposites by presenting herself as a 'satanic woman' in her writings and lectures. Julius Evola would comment on this aspect of her writing in his *Eros and the Mysteries of Love* noting "a deliberate tendency to scandalize the reader through unnecessary dwelling on Satanism."

Maria would be unfettered by the controversy such language caused. The title of her first book and the initial expression of the aims of her order was *La lumière du sexe—rituel d'initiation satanique selon la doctrine du troisième terme de la trinité* (The Light of Sex—Satanic Initiation Ritual According to the Doctrine of the Third Term of the Trinity.) From the outset Maria made it abundantly clear that she would not shy away from embracing the Luciferian aspects of her overtly Satanic feminist vision. It would be impossible to divorce the Satanic elements from her philosophy which was so grounded in the unification of opposites.

In 1929 Maria relocated to Paris but was disappointed to be denied a work permit. Once again left to her own devices, she undertook the project of translating (and some say heavily expanding) American hermeticist, spiritualist, and sex magician Paschal Beverly Randolph's book *Magia Sexualis*. She also began to offer lectures on 'The Third Term of the Trinity' in local cafes and later meeting rooms, presenting her doctrines to the public for the first time.

Attendance to the lectures grew with many notable figures from the art and literary worlds. Occultist and journalist William Seabrook was a student and it has been said that Antonin Artaud, Andre Breton, and Max Ernst were also known to have attended her lectures but documentation of this has yet to surface. It is undeniable that the sexual mysticism of Maria found much common ground with the Surrealists and the two would certainly cross-pollinate ideas. Members of the surrealist group Camille Bryen and Sarane Alexandrian were both part of her circle.

In 1930 Maria announced her new religion - the Third Term of the Trinity, a religion of the Mother whose symbol is the arrow (*La Flèche*), a religion for whom the flesh is the supreme truth of the cosmos and in which the Mother would convert Evil into Good. She would elaborate on this concept in *La Rite Sacre de l'Amour Magique* "The Mother appeases the combat between Christ and Satan in reconciling the two contrary wills under the same vision of unique ascension." This new religion would be explored by her newly founded group of students and initiates, *La Confrérie de la Fèche d'Or.*

In addition to these lectures the Third Term of the Trinity was further spread by in the pages of *La Flèche*, a little newspaper Maria printed up and sold on the streets of Montparnasse. *La Flèche* served as the mouthpiece by which she could spread her ideas and featured articles by her as well as other occultists such as Julius Evola. In these pages, she expanded on themes related to her vision of sexual gnosis as well as topics ranging from Spiritualism, Feminism, Satanism, Masonry and more.

As her popularity and attendance to her salons grew, Maria would expand on her ideas across three original books. Starting in 1932 she released her first original title; *Le Rite Sacre' de l'amour magique*, an allegorical semi-autobiographical novel in which she sought to illustrate her theories of Magical Love. This was followed closely by her most accessible work *La Lumiere du sex* (The Light of Sex) which formed the basis of her instructions for initiates and candidates to *La Confrérie de la Fèche d'Or* (The Brotherhood of the Golden Arrow). Her final book (others were planned but failed to materialize) was *Le Mystère de la Pendaison* which detailed sexual rites involving sensory deprivation as well as an alluring and dangerous ritual of erotic asphyxiation called 'The Hanging Mystery.'

Her work was received with mixed reviews by the esotericists of her time. Some were entranced with this strange beautiful Russian woman with "eyes blue and cold like a glacier ... or rather like the blades of daggers." They were equally fascinated by her new religion of satanic feminism. Others were suspicious. René Guénon wrote a scathing review in *The Veil of Isis* where he accused Maria and La Confrérie de la Fèche d'Or of "suspicious tendencies similar to the Gnostic Church of Lyon." Guénon was perceptive in drawing a line of inspiration and intent from Maria back to the church of Boullan and his successors.

Of the activities of Maria and her group we actually have first-hand contemporary accounts. She was featured in Pierre Geyraud's book *Les Petites Églises De Paris,* interviewed in her room at L'American Hotel. In describing the role of her idealized priestesses Maria explained the means by which the mysteries would be communicated:

> *The Priestess of Love has a job. She must give herself with equal passion to all the men that she arouses. It is not necessary that she love, them, esteem them, or even admire them individually... she gives her body in sacrifice. In this act she must show the same devotion that a nun would show in her religious observances ...the sublime vibrations of this ideal creation awake the man to the revealed wisdom which we call the redeemed Satan or Lucifer.*

In 1935 Maria had a vision in her magic mirror of the catastrophe of World War II and her own imminent demise. Knowing her end was near she refused to reprint her books and called one final gathering of her core students in the Studio Raspail. She informed the attendees that she had completed her mission and the time had come to leave Paris. When pressed by her students she would refuse to name a successor in La Confrérie citing her belief that nothing could be done to spread her works for many generations to come. It was her conviction that only when the world is prepared by social and political upheavals, then could the Third Term of the Trinity be known. Her students were tasked with preserving her teachings and in 1936 she left Paris for the last time.

Maria died on April 17, 1936, in the house of her daughter in Zurich. Having neglected to name a successor, the group dissipated after her departure. It would be many decades before the full import of her legacy would be acknowledged. Increasingly, over the past twenty years, her work has reemerged into the popular consciousness of the occult milieu. For the first time ever her complete works have been translated into English and students now have access to her entire life's work.

Maria may well have been correct in her assessment and the world was not ready for her mission. Perhaps we needed to pass through the conflagration of World War II and the upheavals of the 20th century that opened the way to a cultural and social transformation on the same scale at Paris at the turn of the 19th century. Perhaps now the world is ready for those epiphanies of the Abjected Angel, for those secrets once taught among hunted Gnostics, for those mysteries of blood and sex taught by Sabbath fires, for the masses of the Paraclete and the true power of the priestess. If we are now in that third age, may we be illuminated by the descending dove of Lucifer and her flaming star.

Teachings of the Light

MADELINE MONTALBAN AND THE ORDER OF THE MORNING STAR

Michael Howard

IN AUGUST 1967 I sent a letter to the occult and astrological magazine *Prediction* and asked for it to be forwarded to one of their contributors, 'Madeline Montalban' (Madeline Sylvia Royals 1910–1982). Madeline provided the monthly horoscope forecasts for each issue of the magazine as well as writing feature articles on the Tarot, astrology, magic and folklore. She was born in Blackpool, Lancashire and as a child suffered from polio that left her with a permanent limp. Apparently her paternal grandfather was interested in the occult and introduced her to books to read on the subject while she was bedridden. She also read the Bible avidly and told me that in her opinion the Old Testament was a book of magic and the New Testament a book of mysticism.

After leaving school Madeline studied journalism and in the early 1930s moved to London to be a reporter on the *Daily Express*. While working for the newspaper she was sent to interview Aleister Crowley and is believed to have joined his magical group A∴A∴ or the Order of the Silver Star. After her death one of Madeline's students said he found a set of 'Golden Dawn type robes' in a blanket box in her apartment and these may have belonged to the Order. However she had a poor opinion of the Great Beast and told me he was never a true magician because he could not master astrology properly. During the Second World War Madeline served in the Royal Navy and was on the personal staff of a member of the British royal family, Admiral Lord Louis Mountbatten. She also met and worked magically with the founder of modern Wicca, Gerald Gardner, in the 1940s and edited and typed the manuscript of his occult novel *High Magic's Aid*. After the war she wrote articles for *London Life* magazine before joining *Prediction* in the 1950s.

As a result of the letter I sent to her, Madeline gave me the rare honor of inviting me to visit her apartment in Queen Alexandria Mansions, 3 Grape Street, St Giles Circus in Central London. In the 18th century the St Giles district was a notorious 'rookery' or slum inhabited by thieves, prostitutes and significantly also fortune-tellers, astrologers, alchemists and assorted cunning folk. An occult influence still permeates the area today with the famous Atlantis bookshop, where Madeline briefly worked in the late 1940s, near the British Museum and geographical associations with the Order of the Golden Dawn, the Theosophists, the Swedenborg Society and Freemason's Grand Lodge occupying buildings in the nearby streets at various periods.

At this first meeting in 1967 Madeline and I spent several hours discussing a wide range of esoteric subjects. She evidently recognized something in the shy teenager in front of her. One of the first things she told me was that psychically she could see I had 'the Mark.' At the time this observation puzzled me and it was only later she explained she had seen the 'Mark of Cain' in my aura. This she said appeared on the forehead where the Third Eye or pineal gland was situated, and took the form of a Tau Cross or a pentagram. According to Madeline, the Mark was the recognition symbol of the 'Goodly Company.' These were occult initiates spiritually descended from the Nephelim, the half-human, half-angelic offspring of the marriages between the Watchers and the 'daughters of Cain' mentioned in Genesis. The heraldic symbol of the Tau Cross entwined with a snake was also associated with the motto of Madeline's Luciferian Order of the Morning Star—*In hoc signo vinces* or 'In this sign I conquer.'

In the 1960s, although she was a virtual recluse, Madeline Montalban had the reputation of being 'the greatest magician in London.' However, unlike other magical practitioners of the time who employed Golden Dawn or goetic magic, she drew on a wide range of sources, and underpinning her Art was the Luciferian tradition. Madeline told me her first psychic contact with Lucifer was in 1946 and at that time he passed on his 'secret' name of Lumiel ('Light of God'). It was not until ten years later that Madeline and her partner and soul-mate 'Nicholas Heron' founded the Order of the Morning Star (OMS) together and launched her famous correspondence course in angelic magic.

Nicholas Heron was the pseudonym of a talented engraver, photographer and journalist who worked for a local newspaper called the *Evening Argus* in Brighton, Sussex. He cultivated the persona of an English countryman and has been described as "handsome and charming with good manners." As a writer he also contributed articles to *Prediction* on folk magic, herbalism and druidism. He also produced handcrafted copper talismans for various magical purposes inscribed with the seals and sigils of the planetary sprits. Until he and Madeline parted company in 1964, these talismans were offered for sale to students of the OMS or to the public through advertisements placed in occult magazines.

Madeline and Nicholas Heron ran an occult correspondence course by post as an 'outer court' to the Order based on Madeline's own form of angelic magic. This was offered to readers of *Prediction* who wrote to her about her articles or to the wealthy clients who visited her for personal Tarot readings or astrological advice on the Stock Exchange. The course contained information derived from ancient Chaldean stellar lore, astrology, the Tarot, Gnosticism, the Hermetic tradition and grimoires such as the *Key of Solomon, The Armadel, The Book of Abramelin the Mage,* Agrippa's *Occult Philosophy*, Francis Barrett's *The Magus,* and Dr John Dee's Enochian system.

The Chaldean aspects of magic appealed to Madeline because she believed it was a system based on astrology. She told me that the Chaldean priest-magicians worshipped the stars not as physical objects but as 'visible symbols of invisible forces' that they regarded as the planetary gods. In her system of magical praxis these were transformed into the archangels, possibly because most of the students of her course had Christian backgrounds and could relate easily to these images. Of course through their time in Babylon the Hebrews would have been exposed to the concept of these planetary gods and represented them as angels or the 'messengers of God' who communicated between the Divine and human beings.

The Hermetic element in the course came from the semi-mythical *Book of Thoth* (pronounced Te-hu-ti phonetically in the Egyptian way). This tome had allegedly been translated into Greek from Ancient Egyptian hieroglyphs by a writer called Menetho. He was described as a 'high priest and scribe' from the 'city of the sun', Heliopolis on the River Nile in the 3rd century BCE. *The Book of Thoth* was supposed to have been written after the 'Great Flood', presumably the biblical deluge described in Genesis, by the mythical magus Hermes Trismegistus or Thrice-Greatest. The Hermetic writings entered the European magical and occult tradition in the 15th century when the philosopher Marsilio Ficino translated the *Corpus Hermeticum*. It was subsequently acquired by Cosimo de Medici of the famous Florentine family for his extensive private library.

Madeline regarded the Egyptian god of wisdom Thoth as equivalent to the Greek god Hermes and the Archangel Raphael. To her he was the patron of magicians and identified with the Tarot card known as The Magus or The Magician. One of the names for the Tarot was the *Book of Thoth*. Although the *Corpus Hermeticum* is largely a philosophical work, Madeline taught her students the Hermetic Tradition was expressed in European esotericism as a magical system. It was based on astrology and the belief the destiny of humans was 'written in stars.' In the OMS Hermetic style 'astral magic' was based not only on astrology but also on the medieval doctrine of occult correspondences. These included the symbolic meaning of precious stones and colours, the use of planetary hours and lunar phases, and the invocation of cosmic forces. In Madeline's magical system these 'cosmic forces' were the planetary regents of the solar system or archangels and their leader was Lord Lumiel or Lucifer.

In the practical angelic magic of the OMS Madeline had little time for what she called the 'theatricals' of the type of 'high magic' practised by the groups such as the Golden Dawn. The magical workings I saw her do were simple affairs using small paintings of the archangels, commissioned from one of her students Helger Lucen who was a talented artist, mirrors, colored candles, incense, gold coins, Tarot cards, talismans, magical squares, planetary sigils and virgin parchment on which were written invocations and petitions in the Theban magical alphabet. Knowledge of the lunar phases and daily astrological aspects was required to time magical workings so as to enhance their result by working with the flow of positive cosmic influences. Lucifer and the archangels were called upon in workings to aid the magic.

In an article called 'The Way to Occult Power' published in the *Prediction Annual* of 1969 Madeline described the principles of the Arte Magical as practised in the Order. She said: "Magic teaches us to have power over our own destiny". To do this we must first have power over ourselves, a very Luciferian principle based on individualism. Madeline expressed this process through the term "Man know thyself and thou shalt know the universe and the gods." This involved the would-be magus finding out their purpose in life. In the *Prediction* article Madeline expressed this in Arthurian terms of a medieval knight who after an all-night vigil sets out on a quest to find the Holy Grail. Referring to the sword and chalice on the altar in the Tarot card of The Magician, she identified these as symbols of the contrasexual masculine and feminine aspects of the human psyche–the anima (female) and the animus (male) relating to men and women.

The chalice receives and the sword puts the wisdom received into action. Therefore, according to Madeline's teaching, true magicians are neither wholly male nor female, but on a subtle level a mixture of both. By physical incarnation they may be a man or a woman but mentally and spiritually she believed they were dual beings. She also believed that magic, as an act of creation or bringing spirit into matter, was represented in the Hebrew Cabbala as the *Shekina* or 'Bride of God'. In her teachings it is the 'shining force field of God through which He created' and the 'female side of the Father-Mother God'.

After completing the first half of the correspondence course, the student was offered further lessons outlining teachings regarding the Lightbearer and the 'teaching angels.' Not every student got this far and, because it was such a controversial subject, Madeline decided who would be taken to a further level of knowledge. In the more advanced lessons for senior students of the course, Lucifer is mentioned in the one called *The Book of the Devil*. It follows a description of the hidden symbolism of Baphomet, the goat god of the medieval Order of the Knights Templar, and a list of the 'lost gospels' missing from the New Testament. Madeline first mentions Lucifer as the angel appointed by God or the Cosmic Creator to rule over Earth. She quotes Genesis 1:3–4 which says; 'And God said, Let there be light and there was light' as a reference to Lucifer as the first-born of creation. She also describes Lucifer as the 'first subdivision of God' representing divine knowledge and wisdom and the intellect.

According to the teachings of the OMS, Lucifer was frustrated at the slow evolution of the primitive human race, described as 'furless monkeys', and therefore the angels 'mingled their vibrations' with the 'daughters of earth'. Unfortunately humanity was not evolved enough to use the power they were given by this process and misused it leading to chaos and anarchy. In *The Book of the Devil*, the Cosmic Creator says Lumiel must redeem himself for his error of judgement by becoming the 'Light of the World.' In that role he must incarnate in human form and in his 'coat of skin' sacrifice himself and take on 'all the pains and sorrows your mistakes have brought to humanity.'

Controversially, Madeline was revealing to her students that one of these periodic incarnations was as the Christ, who was the 'Light of the World' and died on the cross for the 'sins' of the human race. In this respect she refers in the lesson to Revelation 22:16 where Jesus says: "I am the root and offspring of David, and the bright and morning star." These words indicate that the spirit of Lucifer, symbolised by the 'morning star' Venus, as the Christos or 'anointed one' is incarnated in or overshadows the physical body of Jesus of Nazareth, the scion of the royal house of King David and heir to the Jewish throne. This is why when he is captured in the Garden of Gethsemane the armed followers of Jesus briefly and violently resist the temple guards (Matthew 26:51–52). As far as they were concerned they were fighting for the true heir to the royal throne usurped by the puppet king Herod installed by the Roman occupation forces. Other incarnations of Lucifer on Earth mentioned by Madeline included the Greek god Dionysus and the 'fathered serpent' Quetzalcoatl worshipped by the Aztecs. To these can be added Adonis and Attis and any sacrificed saviour god in history.

If their reaction to this sensational revelation about Lumiel and the Christ was not a negative one, the student might be invited to learn more and enter the OMS. My personal copy of a further lesson *The Book of Lumiel: The Incredible Archangel of Earth* is clearly marked 'For the Members of the Order of the Morning Star.' In the introduction Madeline says she first began to research the story of Lucifer in 1944 and, as with most of her magical and occult knowledge, she found it initially in museums and libraries. She begins by saying that because women were held in such low esteem in the Middle East, a patriarchal priesthood presented the serpent (Lucifer) in the Garden of Eden myth as an evil being seducing the first woman Eve and leading her astray. However, as a proto-feminist, Madeline says the reason for this was that Lucifer had contacted Eve and not the clay-born Adam. She adds that women are 'peculiarly attuned to the receiving of angelic information' and 'Lumiel prefers priestesses to priests.'

Following the introduction to the lesson is what Madeline claims is an English translation from the angelic Enochian language of a text written on the so-called 'Tablet of Light' relating Lucifer's story. My personal opinion is that this document is based on the psychic contact Madeline claimed to have had with Lumiel in the 1940s and included information gleaned from other sources. This would explain some of the contradictions in the material. It is written as a personal account by Lucifer who begins by stating that the Cosmic Creator is responsible for many universes but he

(Lucifer) is the first being created in this one. This comment predicts the findings of modern quantum physicists who talk about the 'multiverse' or the theory that the universe we inhabit is only one of many.

Lucifer then says the Cosmic Creator is dual natured, the perfection of male and female in one divine being, and divided into the Divine Mother (*Shekinah*), his twin and partner. After this primary division came the birth of Lucifer and then further subdivisions of the Divine followed creating the 'sons of God' or archangels. They were appointed as the rulers of the planets in the solar system—the sun (Michael), Mercury (Raphael), Venus (Anael), Earth (Lumiel), the moon (Gabriel), Mars (Samael), Jupiter (Scahiel), Saturn (Cassiel), Uranus (Uriel), Neptune (Asariel) and Pluto (Azrael). These planetary angelic correspondences broadly relate to those listed in Barrett's *The Magus,* which was one of Madeline's important source books. One idea is that originally Lumiel was the solar logos or regent of the sun. After his Fall from Heaven, when he became the 'Lord of the World', Lucifer was appointed as the planetary regent of Terra or Earth. When he is redeemed he will take his proper role in the cosmic plan and once more will be the solar archangel.

The Book of Lumiel seems to accept the theory of evolution because it describes how humans developed from 'the first primitive forms of life' (amoebas) on Earth. However there were other pre-human life forms of a spiritual nature, who were created perfect and were not intended to have physical bodies, known as the Ray People or Ray Children. They were destined to be the supreme race on Earth to assist Lumiel in his responsibility for the development of the human race. The Cosmic Plan was for the early humans to be at first the servants of the Ray People and then in time become their equals. The spiritualized humans would then be absorbed into the Ray People, become angelic and be united with the Body of Light of the Cosmic Creator.

As imaginatively depicted in the sci-fi movie *2001: A Space Odyssey* based on a novella by Arthur C. Clarke, ultimately humans would be reborn as a 'star child' or archangels who would rule planets in this or the other universes. In Madeline's Luciferian teachings the original Adam and Eve were of the nature of the Ray People and the Garden of Eden existed on the spiritual plane. In that sense their banishment from paradise was a fall from spirit to matter and incarnation in physical bodies (see Genesis 3:21). The point where the first couple suddenly became aware of their nakedness was when they abandoned their spiritual forms for 'coats of skin'. The pattern of what life on Earth would be was formatted by Lumiel on this astral level before becoming a physical reality on the material plane after millions of years of evolution.

In the second part of *The Book of Lumiel,* allegedly based on another 'Tablet of Light,' the text is represented as part of a conversation between the Lightbearer and 'a priestess of the secret cult.' Lumiel describes how he opposed the Cosmic Plan and attempted to accelerate what he saw as the slow pace of human evolution by direct intervention. This led to the separation of the angelic host into two opposing camps or factions supporting either Michael, appointed as the 'Defender of the Plan' by God, and Lucifer leading the rebellion against it. At the end of this part of the lesson Madeline summarises the contents and says the biblical Edenic myth is an allegory representing the male phallic urge. She also says the union with the fallen angels caused humans to split into warring tribes. As a result an earthly ruler called Jehovah or Yahweh attempted to enforce draconian laws and religious and cultural taboos to restore law and order after the Flood. Lumiel was also demoted by the followers of the patriarchal religions from his angelic status to become the mythical Satan, originally a collective name for minor angels sent by God to test the faithful (see the Book of Job). Influenced by the dualistic Manichean heresy, the Early Church transformed Satan into a cosmic principle of evil seeking to wrest the souls of humanity from God.

The Book of Lumiel concludes with a short extract from the so-called 'Michael Tablet' that totally subverts the story of the War in Heaven. It states that Michael and Lumiel were never enemies, although they disagreed on matters of divine policy. After the Fall it says the Archangel Michael took the green and purple banner of Lumiel and showed it to the angelic host referring to the Lightbearer as his brother. He said that Lumiel had symbolically gone into the darkness "yet the Light of Heaven and the Light of the Universe are indissoluble" for there "must be light and darkness". While his angelic brother's light had set for a while, Lumiel would survive as the star of the morning, which heralds the ascent of the sun at dawn. Michael adds that the "Lion of the Sun and the Dragon of Darkness" are the two sides of one coin and that Lumiel's return is awaited "when the minds of men and women are illumined by the truth." This reflects other Luciferian teachings found in other traditions that represent Lucifer and Michael as twins or different aspects of the same cosmic force. Madeline summed this non-dualistic unity up with the saying: "The light is in the darkness and the darkness is in the light."

Although Madeline claimed her Luciferian teachings were based on research and her psychic contacts with Lumiel, I believe there were other sources that influenced them. One of the subjects Madeline and I discussed at our first meeting in August 1967 was the mythical lost continent of Atlantis. In common with most occultists of her generation, Madeline was a firm believer in the ancient physical existence of Atlantis and accepting of all matters of an Atlantean nature. I must admit it was a subject we politely agreed to disagree on. The lost continent featured in her teachings because she insisted all members of the Order of the Morning Star had shared incarnations in the priesthoods of Ancient Egypt and Atlantis, who were historically and esoterically linked.

Madeline claimed that high ranking Atlantean magical adepts became aware by divination or spirit contact that the great island in the Atlantic Ocean was to be destroyed in a natural cataclysm. This would be engineered by the Gods because its priest-kings, the ruling power elite and scientists had indulged in unnatural and unethical acts. These included 'black magic' and the artificial mating of humans with animals to create a bestial 'slave race' in a form of genetic engineering. Allegedly the Atlantean scientists had also invented 'super weapons of mass destruction' that threatened the whole world.

According to Madeline, 'good' Atlantean adepts secretly left the island in fleets of specially built boats called 'arks'. These refugees set up colonies in South America, North Africa and the British Isles, hence the similarity between the pyramids and ancient megalithic monuments found in these places. Because the Atlantean adepts were spiritually and technologically more advanced then the primitive people they encountered they acted as teachers and cultural exemplars. As a result the indigenous races regarded them as divine beings and they were transformed into gods and goddesses.

In Ancient Egypt the examples of this process given to me by Madeline were the creator god Ptah, Isis and her brother/husband Osiris and the magician Thoth. In the writings of the 20th century occultist Dion Fortune and her students Christine Hartley and Gareth Knight the Atlanteans who fled to Britain are identified as Arthur, Merlin and Morgan Le Fay. Gareth Knight claims they were also of faery origin and were of the bloodline of the royal house of Atlantis. As such they introduced this genetic legacy into the ancient British race. Knight bases this claim on spirit communications received through the mediumship of Dion Fortune and after her death in 1946 Margaret Lumley Brown.

It was only after I had met Madeline and became a student of her Order that I came across a series of books written in the 1920s by an English psychic and occultist High C. Randall-Stevens, also known as 'El Eros.' By profession he was a singer but in 1925 claimed to have heard a spirit voice who dictated a series of teachings to him over the next year that collectively were known as the Osirian Scripts. The spirit who contacted Randall-Stevens was supposed to be an initiate in Ancient Egypt and his messages described the creation of the human race, the esoteric Egyptian Mysteries, the destruction of Atlantis and predicted that it might be repeated today.

In 1954 H.C. Randall-Stevens founded the Order of Knights Templars of Aquarius (sic) on Jersey in the Channel Islands to promote the teachings. Its aim was to prevent the descent of humanity into gross materialism owing to the decline of spirituality and spiritual values in the modern world. The Order's members recognised the power of thought for both personal and planetary healing. They sought to guide humankind on to a path leading to spiritual enlightenment and eventual union with what they called the Father-Mother God or the Cosmic Creator. Interestingly the Osirian Scripts refer to a pre-Adamic race associated with Atlantis called the Ray People or Ray Children who existed on a spiritual level. When the island was destroyed the spirit communications describe how the Atlanteans colonised Central and South America and Egypt. They were greeted as civilisers and later deified.

Whether it is accepted as an actual physical reality or just as an allegorical myth, what does Atlantis represent on a spiritual and philosophical level? There are obvious connections and associations with certain forms and interpretations of the Luciferian traditions and some of its composite elements. The Atlantean legend encapsulates the primeval myth of a 'Golden Age' and an earthly paradise and its demise, the descent of spiritual beings into matter, cultural exemplars who taught early human the arts and crafts of civilisation, occult knowledge and the magical arts and were transformed into divinities, and a universal cataclysm remembered in the Bible and other Middle Eastern accounts as a Great Flood when a hero by divine guidance saved the human race from total extinction. All these aspects are to be found in the Luciferian teachings of Madeline Montalban and her Order of the Morning Star.

'Non Serviam' as Ontological Paradigm

LUCIFER, PROMETHEUS AND THE SPIRIT OF REBELLION IN MODERN MAGIC

Frater U∴D∴

THE MYTHICAL FIGURE of Lucifer has long served Christian iconology as a placeholder for Satan and everything evil, heretical and inadmissible. From there, its general usage has percolated right into present day political-speak, as witness the claim, reported by the *Guardian* and other media, of former US Republican House speaker John Boehner regarding presidential candidate Ted Cruz in the 2016 primaries: 'Ted Cruz is "Lucifer in the flesh".'[1] Of course, what may come over as a more or less amusing example of pop culture assimilating formerly popular terms and concepts of a predominantly religious mindset today, it was actually a deadly serious concept historically in both the figurative as well as the literal sense.

Literally termed 'the shining one', the 'bringer of light' or 'bringer of dawn' by the Greeks, Lucifer's predecessor Eosphorus (Ἑωσφόρος, Eosphoros) who alternatively went by the names Heosphorus/Heosphoros or Phosphorus (Φωσφόρος, Phosphoros) was, as is well known, the morning star or the planet Venus (actually, Venus is the latinised name for Greek

1 'Ted Cruz is "Lucifer in the flesh", says former speaker John Boehner'. http://www.theguardian.com/us-news/2016/apr/29/ted-cruz-is-lucifer-in-the-flesh-says-former-speaker-john-boehner. Accessed on 29 April, 2016.

Aphrodite). He was the son of Titans, namely Eos and her spouse Astraios, his siblings being the four winds Boreas, Notos, Euros, and Zephyros. He is mentioned in Homer's *Ilias*,[2] in Hesiod's *Theogony*[3] and on multiple occasions in the *Dyonisiaca* ascribed to Nonnus of Pannos.[4]

Originally, the early Greeks erroneously dissociated the planet Venus from the 'evenstar' Hesperos (Ἕσπερος), treating them as separate entities both astronomically as well as in their mythology. After this mistaken assumption was rectified, they nevertheless retained their habit of distinguishing between the two in mythology and poetry, making for plenty of genealogical confusion. While this fact goes to show that Eosphorus was imbued with a certain amount of ambiguity (dawn/dusk) right from the start, it shall be of no further concern to us here.

Eosphorus's mother Eos (Ἠώς), whom the Romans were later to venerate as Aurora, had been around even in pre-Hellenic times: sister of the sun god Helios and of Selene (the moon), she was herself regarded as goddess of the moon, and of magic. She was also notorious for her promiscuous behaviour. Her father was Hyperion, the 'One Above' and yet another 'bringer of light' within this illuminated genealogy. Heralded by the morning star, she was also revered as the genetrix of all the stars and planets.

In ancient Rome, Eosphorus was translated to 'Lucifer' which is, of course, simply the Latin version of the Greek term, meaning 'light bringer' (from *lux*, 'light', and *ferre*, 'to bring'). Here again he is the morning star or Venus (as juxtaposed for Greek Aphrodite).

Turning to the judeo-christian cultural context, we find in Isaiah 14:12: 'How art thou fallen from heaven, O Lucifer, son of the morning! how art thou cut down to the ground, which didst weaken the nations!'[5] Here, the Hebrew *hêlêl* (הֵילֵל) which translates as 'shining one, light bearer', rendered as Heosphoros (i.e. 'bringer of dawn') in the Greek *Septuagint*, is derived directly from the Latin *Vulgate* which translates it as *lucifer* i.e. 'light bearer' or, again, the morning star Venus.

There is quite a bit of doubt amongst scholars that the 'fallen morning star' addressed here actually connotes an angel or some other divine entity

2 Homer, *Ilias*, 23,226.

3 Hesiod, *Theogony*, 381.

4 Nonnus, *Dyonisiaca*, 6, 18, 44, 138, 299.

5 King James Version (KJV), Isaiah 14:12.

as popular wisdom will have it. Rather, the verse has generally come to be regarded as the prophet's taunt against the (unnamed) king of Babylon.[6]

There is also some indication that the trope of the fallen morning star stems from Canaanite mythology: it was the god Attar, who tried to dethrone the god Baal, failing which he was forced to descend into the underworld.[7] Most likely this myth in turn was based upon an earlier narrative in which Helel, a lesser god in the Canaanite pantheon, attempted to dethrone the northern mountain deity El.[8] What is particularly interesting about these references is the very early connection we find here between Lucifer (in actual fact his precursors) and the spirit of insubordination and rebellion. It is this aspect of Lucifer's contrarian, non-conformist attitude that we are focusing on here.

The final demonisation of Lucifer from a Christian point of view was perpetrated by Origen of Alexandria, who, in his *De principiis Prooemium*, was the first to equate Lucifer with the biblical Satan or Devil. Here, Lucifer in his pride equates himself with God Almighty and is consequently relegated–the fallen angel as we have come to know him since. Other church fathers such as Tertullian, Cyprian, and Ambrosius, to mention only the most influential, seconded this view and thus contributed to its continued propagation.[9]

In scriptural terms, this interpretation was based on Luke 10:18: 'And he said unto them, I beheld Satan as lightning fall from heaven.'[10] In the early medieval church it was then fortified and developed into a veritable dogma. From this point on, Lucifer would stand for heresy incarnate, the epitome of the antinomian, subversive spirit so obnoxious to the advocates of orthodoxy. Or, as the powers that were (and those that still are) would

6 For the image of the 'fallen' morning star Lucifer as a taunt against the dead king of Babylon, see amongst others: James D. G. Dunn and John W. Rogerson, eds. *Eerdmans commentary on the Bible*, Grand Rapids, Mich.: Eerdmans, 2003, p. 511.

7 John Day, *Yahweh and the Gods and Goddesses of Canaan*, Journal for the Study of the Old Testament. Supplement series 265. London, New York: Sheffield Academic Press, 2002.

8 See Gary V. Smith, *Isaiah 1-39, The New American Commentary* 15 A. Nashville Tenn.: B & H Publ. Group, 2007 and Marvin H. Pope, *EL in the Ugaritic Texts*, Vetus Testamentum Suppl 2. Leiden: Brill, 1955.

9 For a more detailed overview of the various iterations the Luciferian motif was subjected to, see Ernst Osterkamp, *Lucifer: Stationen eines Motivs*, Komparatistische Studien 9. Berlin: De Gruyter, 1979.

10 King James Version (KJV), Luke 10:18.

have it: the embodiment of pure hubris and arrogance of a formerly ultra-privileged creature.

This dovetails neatly with another ancient myth of rebellion, to be specific that of Prometheus. This Titan (whose name, incidentally, translates as 'forethought') was seen as the creator of mankind and its greatest benefactor. Interestingly, one of his sobriquets was Pyrphoros (Πυρφόρος) or 'fire bringer', a very obvious parallel to Eosphoros/Lucifer. Bringer of light, bringer of fire—if nothing else this alone would suffice to equate the two with each other.

But there is more. As with most common myths, various–occasionally conflicting–versions abound. And once again it is Hesiod[11] who contributes the most common narrative though we can observe varying takes in the writings of Homer, Pindar and Pythagoras as well. In a nutshell, Prometheus steals the fire from heaven (actually from mount Olympus, abode of the gods) to empower mankind, promoting human survival and enabling the establishment of civilisation as we know it. This is conducted against the express will of Zeus who subsequently condemns Prometheus to eternal punishment: he is chained to a mountain where he is bedevilled daily by Zeus, symbolised by an eagle, who devours his liver. Due to his immortality, this vital organ (which, let's not forget, the Greeks took to be the physical abode of the soul) is regenerated every night.[12]

It wasn't only the major Athenian dramatists Aeschylus, Sophocles and Euripides who were deeply influenced by this myth. Indeed, it was to leave its mark on Western literature and art in its entirety from the Renaissance on well into the 20th century, two of the best known literary works being Percy Bysshe Shelley's drama *Prometheus Unbound* (1820) as well as his wife's, Mary Wollstonecraft Shelley's novel *Frankenstein; or, The Modern Prometheus* (1823).

Rather than delve into ever more mythological and historical minutiae, suffice it to summarise that both figures, Lucifer and Prometheus, while quite arguably not entirely identical, are united by a great number of common features. Firstly there is the defiant spirit of subversion and rebellion against the world as is. However, contrary to the claims of orthodox Christian theology, this is not about 'evil' per se: rather, it is the projection of a gnostic impulse countering mere belief (as in 'we'll assume things are probably so and so, though we don't—and probably never can—really know for sure') and the suspension of resultant skeptical disbelief (e.g. in the Jesuits' *reservatio mentalis*) with a salvific revelatory knowledge (as opposed to mere intellectual raciocination) that has never been catered to let alone adopted by the forces of conventional reality production. Thus, Lucifer's infamous *non serviam* ('I shall not serve') does not stay limited to its original theological context. This goes to explain both why and how Prometheus and Lucifer were finally merged when reflected by secular, by rational and by a number of spiritual, metaphysical schools of thought.

11 Hesiod, *Theogony*, 507–616. Furthermore, in *Works and Days*, 42–105.

12 It is only many years later that Heracles, the Greek hero, slays the eagle and finally frees Prometheus from his torment.

The French Revolution's slogan (which was to be adopted by the anarchist movement in later years) *ni dieu ni maître* ('[let there be] neither god nor master') is, if nothing else, a direct implementation of this contrarian attitude as projected onto the realm of revolutionary politics.

In a more marginalised manner maybe not subscribed to by the majority of Western magical authors, this merger of Prometheus and Lucifer actually encompasses Satan as well even to the extent that for instance Anton Szandor LaVey's original *First Church of Satan*, arguable the most seminal prototype of modern day satanism, omits to distinguish between the three.[13] Again, there are precedents. H. P. Blavatsky's Theosophy[14] views the 'fall of Lucifer' as a descent of light into matter, its spiritualisation imbuing it with divine consciousness: an act of enlightenment akin to the gnostics' view of the snake's role in paradise as narrated in Genesis.

Theosophy's schismatic child, Rudolf Steiner's Anthroposophy, adopts a much more complex view we cannot delve into in greater detail here.[15] By way of a very brief summary, Lucifer is viewed as the opponent of Ahriman, incorporating a spiritual force responsible for intellectuality and visionary imagination—including, it need be said, delusion. One of the peculiarities of the anthroposophical view being the fact that, according to Steiner, Lucifer was actually incarnated as a human being about 3000 BCE in China.

One of the most influential modern works informing the popular view of Lucifer/Satan as a harbinger of enlightenment and human liberation from the strictures of bourgeois social mores and morals are undoubtedly Charles Baudelaire's *Les litanies de Satan* ('The Litanies of Satan'), part of his then-scandalous anthology *Les fleurs du mal* ('The Flowers of Evil') published originally in various extended and reduced editions (both censored

13 LaVey, Anton S., *The Satanic Bible*, [repr.]. New York: Avon Books, 1969.

14 For a brief online overview of Theosophy's interpretation see: 'Lucifer the Lightbringer'. Accessed 30 April, 2016. https://blavatskytheosophy.com/lucifer-the-light-bringer/.

15 A comprehensive summary (in German) can be found online here: 'Luzifer.' Accessed 30 April, 2016. http://anthrowiki.at/Luzifer. For a somewhat briefer introduction in English see: 'Lucifer'. Accessed 30 April, 2016. https://sites.google.com/site/waldorf-watch/lucifer.

and not) between 1857 and in its final version (posthumously) 1868. Here, conventional Christianity's view of things is inverted and Satan is adored as the embodiment of enlightened knowledge. Obviously, Baudelaire's work is part and parcel of a long literary tradition (still ongoing) focusing on Lucifer/Satan who is sometimes depicted as the epitome of sheer hubris, pride and arrogance, at other times in the gnostic tradition as the redeemer from a world governed by an usurpatory pseudo-deity (Demiurge, Jehovah, Ialdabaoth, Saklas etc.).

To name but a few other literary examples: Dante Alighieri's *Inferno* (1321), *Doctor Faustus* by Christopher Marlowe (1604), *Paradise Lost* by John Milton (1667), Johann Wolfgang von Goethe's *Faust* (1808-1832), William Blake's *The Marriage of Heaven and Hell* (1790–1793), Nathaniel Hawthorne's *The Scarlet Letter* (1850), Herman Melville's *Moby Dick* (1851), William Golding's *Lord of the Flies* (1954), Lawrence Durrell's *Monsieur or the Prince of Darkness* (1974), *Earthly Powers* by Anthony Burgess (1980), Salman Rushdie's *Satanic Verses* (1988)...and the list goes on.

Returning briefly to Baudelaire's poem, it features a closing prayer that is quite descriptive of the 'darker' approach to modern magic without necessarily being identical with full fledged one-dimensional Satanism proper (translation mine):[16]

PRAYER
Glory and praise to you, Satan, in the heights
Of Heaven where you reigned, and in the depths
Of Hell where, vanquished, you dream in silence!
Grant that my soul may someday repose under the Tree of Knowledge,
near to you, at the time when, over your brow,
Like a new Temple its branches will spread!

Admittedly, the compounding of Lucifer, Satan and Prometheus as an essentially identical entity briefly sketched above is problematic from

16 In the French original:
PRIÈRE
Gloire et louange à toi, Satan, dans les hauteurs
Du Ciel, où tu régnas, et dans les profondeurs
De l'Enfer, où, vaincu, tu rêves en silence!
Fais que mon âme un jour, sous l'Arbre de Science,
Près de toi se repose, à l'heure où sur ton front
Comme un Temple nouveau ses rameaux s'épandront!

a mythological and historical view, resulting in endless furious disputes both in academe and in the world of occultism. However, this purist type of discourse typically misses one important point: occult philosophy and its mythologemes have always been fundamentally eclecticist. Rather than viewing this as one of its main liabilities, as is so common within the academic realm, I personally see it as its chief asset. Occultism has always refused to hold rigidly to any given single paradigm or set of assumptions as prescribed by societal convention. Instead, occultism—and by inference magic—has drawn upon a plethora of varying, sometimes even flagrantly contradictory, theories, ideas and modes of operation. Not for want of a unifying theoretical superstructure or *oberbau*, but recurring to an entirely pragmatic craving to gain complementary insights into whatever area it happens to be delving into.

Unsurprisingly, this approach will often shun standardised conventions or rules dictating which theories are to be combined and in which particular manner. It is true that the eclectic mode more often than not may seem to lack consistency of thinking, that it may call for more elegance and simplicity. But this is actually indistinguishable from any empirical approach. While undoubtedly there have always been plenty of utterly dogmatic black-or-white schools of thoughts bedeviling the occult current as a whole, this should not distract us from the fact that all occultists, be they professed magicians or metaphysicians of whatever ilk, have always been (and continue to be) a tiny minority surviving within an essentially unfriendly if not downright hostile social environment. This makes them contrarians by definition, regardless of whether they want to be (or view themselves as such) or not. If you're an atheist or an agnostic living in a rigidly religious environment, a polytheist amongst monotheists, an alchemist in the midst of conventional chemists—there will always be some fundamental tensions to deal with and, in a worst case scenario—*vide* the persecution of witches, heretics and dissenters in not-too-recent Western history—to survive.

Nor does this mean to imply that partaking of any given minority view of things automatically makes you 'right' or entitles you to some privileges in any way. The world is full of inanely mistaken minority know-it-alls and smart-arses and both occultism in general and magic in particular are no exception. But realising the overall societal minority status magicians are adopting by default does underline their intrinsic affinity to any antagonistic *weltanschauung* opposed if not persecuted by the powers of convention.

Investigating Germany's oldest magical order, the *Fraternitas Saturni* [FS] (of which I have been a member for over 30 thirty years), we can see this approach in action.[17] Before we proceed, however, let it be noted that in spite of what its name implies the FS isn't focused on Saturn alone. Rather, it is involved in promoting the 'Saturnian-Uranian' era which may go to explain its rather surprising, unorthodox equating of Saturn, the 'Guardian of the Threshhold', with Lucifer. As the order's founder Gregor A. Gregorius wrote [translation mine]:

> *Lucifer as morning star [...] isn't merely the fallen great angel Lucifer but also the brother of Christ. Saturn in his highest octave is deepest wisdom incarnate concerning maturation via suffering. Salvation awaits even behind his dark gate.*[18]

It doesn't end there, however. Gregorius based his views of the dichotomy Sol/Saturn on a cosmosophical speculation according to which the planets are destined to clash and merge with each other at some point in time.[19] In this manner, the egocentric power of the solar demiurge will be smashed by the Saturnian Lucifer principle, thereby liberating humankind from the gods' paternalism and dominance. Once again Gegrorius [translation mine]:

> *However, once Saturn returns to the Sun, once the two have become a giant double star having absorbed all the other planets to circle the sky in loneliness, Saturn rejoins with Christ, and the end of our cosm will be near again. In all probability, Saturn will prove to be the stronger one. This dark angel's*

17 For a generally accurate if somewhat dated English overview of the *Fraternitas Saturni* see: Flowers, Stephen E., *Fire and Ice: Magical Teachings of Germany's Greatest Secret Occult Order,* Llewellyn's Teutonic Magick series. St. Paul, MN, USA: Llewellyn, 1990. Stephen and I had been in contact for a while before and when he conducted his research for this book I assisted him with some internal information and personal comments at the time inasmuch as my vows of secrecy permitted me to do so.

18 Gregorius, Gregor A., 'Das göttliche negative Prinzip', *Blätter für angewandte okkulte Lebenskunst*, Berlin, March 1954. In the German original: 'Luzifer als Morgenstern [...] ist nicht nur der gefallene große Engel Luzifer, sondern auch der Bruder von Christus. Saturn in seiner höchsten Oktave ist verkörpertes tiefstes Wissen um die Reife durch das Leid. Auch hinter seinem dunklen Tore steht die Erlösung.'

19 Gregorius, Gregor A. 'Das System der planetarischen Sphären', *Blätter für angewandte okkulte Lebenskunst*, Berlin, September 1951.

> *atomistic structure is, as far as his inner core is concerned, denser and more compact by far than the solar body (lead and gold), which makes it likely that at the end of the planetary evolution Saturn may be devoured by the Sun, but only to dominate and redeem the Sun as a purged, liberated and redeemed principle.*[20]

While the official FS as an organisation may no longer subscribe to this particular brand of cosmosophy, the concept of an essentially Luciferian Saturn Gnosis prevails. Constituting an eclectic melting pot of various occult currents and schools of thought from its very inception, the FS has undergone a phase of conducting explicitly Luciferian ritual operations mainly in the 1990s, as pushed by its then grandmaster. This focused primarily on the 'non serviam' aspect of the Lucifer archetype. Dedicated work on Luciferian gnosis has been somewhat toned down in the recent past but its influence is still alive and kicking unabatedly.

The above is merely a brief sketch of what is in effect a highly complex and multi faceted phenomenon pertaining to Lucifer. Let us summarise and identify further interesting areas awaiting closer research. Legitimately equating (at least in significant parts) Lucifer with Prometheus, based on both archetypes' perceived agenda of empowering humanity in its struggle against ignorant/blind/evil deities, much more is to be found. This includes occult currents such as mid to late 19th century French Satanism (Joris-Karl Huysmans, Joséphin 'Sâr Merodach' Péladan, Stanislas de Guaïta and others); Austin Osman Spare (as in his basing magic on Freud's psychoanalysis and his inversion of the Viennese psychologist's theory of repression and subconscious complexes in constructing his sigil magic); Aleister Crowley's Scientific Illuminism as well as his ecstatic cult of Pan; German occultists (beginning with the mythical Dr Faust), Stanislaw Przybyszewski (*Die Synagoge Satans*, 'Satan's Synagogue'), Rah-Omir Quintscher (battery magic, and more), Bardon's scientistic focus

20 Gregorius, Gregor A., 'Über den Hüter der Schwelle', *Blätter für angewandte okkulte Lebenskunst*, Berlin, March 1954. In the German original: 'Wenn aber Saturn zur Sonne zurückkehren wird, wenn beide als riesiges Doppelgestirn, das alle die anderen Planeten in sich aufgenommen hat, einsam am Himmel kreisen, Sat-mit Christus wieder verbunden steht, ist das Ende unseres Kosmos wieder nahe. Voraussichtlich ist Saturn der Stärkere. Dieser dunkle Engel ist in seiner atomistischen Struktur, was seinen innersten Kern anbetrifft, weitaus dichter und kompakter als der Sonnenkörper (Blei und Gold), sodaß am Ende der Planeten-Evolution wohl Saturn von der Sonne verschlungen wird, aber dann als geläutertes, befreites und erlöstes Prinzip die Sonne beherrscht und erlöst.'

on electro-magnetism, my own promotion of Pragmatic Magic; Israel Regardie's, Dion Fortune's, William Gray's and David Conway's recourse to depth psychology; the Fraternitas Saturni's specific brand of Saturn Gnosis; the attempts (however amateurish) of Peter J. Carroll at consolidating Chaos Magic with quantum physics (just as the reductionist redefinition of trance as 'gnosis')—there is truly plenty of scope to analyse these occultural phenomena in greater depth.

Also, in post-structuralist, deconstructionist and generally postmodern magic Lucifer has (retro-)mutated from a salvific 'bearer of light/knowledge/wisdom/empowerment' to an antinomian, anarchic archetype of rebellion and iconoclasm versus established wisdom, institutions and societal power structures. Within a philosophical and ideological context the 'I shall not serve [anyone]' has ramified into 'I shall not take anything for granted', thereby tying up what started out in antiquity as a metaphysical and cosmogonical school of thought with the basic tenets of the Age of Enlightenment, of Reason as well as Rationalism. While many though not all of these developments may legitimately be termed '(neo-)gnostic', their common denominator is the fact that they are all ultimately based on Luciferian precepts.

Thus it comes as no surprise that Gnosticism and its modern day (predominantly secular) offspring are still very much the bogeymen of conventional Christian theology, be it Roman Catholic, Protestant or Orthodox. At the end of the day, it is still the concept of *knowledge* vs. *faith* (in gnostic terms: *gnosis* vs. *pistis*) and the empowerment of mankind vs. its servitude to an alien deity (what Christian theologians are wont to revile as man's 'self-deification') that defines this age-old conflict.

As it happens, in my *High Magic* I myself have written a short piece on 'The Magician Lucifer' which doubles as a basic introduction to the fundamentally radical antinomian approach of *Ice Magic*.[21] By way of a parting note, I have included it below in full length.

21 Frater U∴D∴, *eismagie: erste einblicke*, Bad Münstereifel: Edition Magus im Verlag Ralph Tegtmeier, 1996. [This book is still only available in German, an English edition being yet in the making.] While Ice Magic makes no specific mention of either Gnosticism, Lucifer or Prometheus, it definitely incorporates the associated mode of fundamental criticism of all existential tenets and the very foundations of conventional views of magic.

[*Note*: The following quote from my book[22] is, in its entirety, anything but verbatim as I have amended several translation errors and inaccuracies, some of which seriously distorted parts of my message as presented in the German original text. This, therefore, is the first definitive English version to be published. For the sake of uniformity, American spelling has been preserved throughout.]

MAGIC OR THE UNFINISHED LEGEND OF THE MAGICIAN LUCIFER

And God saw the light, that it was good: and God divided the light from the darkness. (Genesis 1:41)

And when We said to the angels: Make obeisance to Adam they all did obeisance but Iblis. He refused out of pride, and he became an unbeliever. (The Koran, 2nd Surah, v. 341)

Lucifer was the most beautiful of the angels. And he was God's favorite, too, until one day he shot his '*Non serviam!*' at him, his definitive declaration of disobedience. The 'fall' of Lucifer was indeed an act of resignation, a retirement. With one single act of resistance he unmasked the power structures behind the purportedly so 'well-meaning' father of creation–there was no room for rebellion, paradise could only exist based on submission, the conformation of its inhabitants to a 'happiness' that, in Lucifer's eyes, was nothing but a pale reflection of that which 'creation' (which he now recognized as being 'uncreated') was capable of at the most. The mere act of establishing one single god had already informed irrevocably for all time the trajectory which 'creation' was to follow into its dead-end terminal, its tenets being the rule of power over powerlessness, the strong over the weak, the proteins over the silicates.

Magic is the path of power, the ability to exert influence. Power means access, having hold of things; it means that there is no more gap between being and consciousness, between subject and object, between hunter and prey. Only one side can prevail. There are only two paths to choose from—the path of adaptation or the other one. Why is it so vaguely referred to as 'the other one'? Because humanity thus far has pursued the path of adaptation for hundreds of thousands of years and because even our very

22 Frater U.·.D.·., *High Magic II: Expanded Theory & Practice,* Woodbury: Llewellyn Publications, 2008, pp. 235–238.

language is an expression of this need for orientation and our adaptation to the outside, to the inside, to the alien, to the peril—a remnant from a time when man had already lost his freedom to say either yes or no. For most people, this question has been decided long ago and it will never be posed again as the course of development has turned everyone once and for all into yea-sayers.

Magic is the path of struggle and of occupying space: the struggle against being denied grasp, hold, access to nature, society, and religion; the struggle for the power to gain hold over the laws of nature, over the development of society, and of freedom. A civilized person is by nature and disposition a predator; his or her god is acquisition and accumulation by breaking the spells of the world and blunting the demands of the Greek gifts of freedom and fire. Civilization is the technology of adapting to the forces of gravity and of cold, to heat and to the seasons, to light and darkness, to life and death. Civilization administrates need, lack and fear, and it summarizes these under the glossy title of 'reality' and 'provision.' No escape has been provided for. Not in the realm of nature: humans cannot fly. ('Or can they?' the magician asks, and tries it out himself/herself.) Not in the realm of society: a non-conformist will be declared crazy and locked away. (But does not 'craziness' imply 'standing on the sidelines' and no longer participating in that old fool's farce of salvation? asks the magician–and cultivates his or her own craziness.) Not in the realm of religion: a non-conformist threatens the monopoly of access to transcendence, as transcendence is 'that which leads us beyond limitation.' (The magician proclaims: 'I don't want anything to do with a god whose power is based on the collaboration of spiritual receptionists,' and thus creates his or her own gods.)

If Lucifer the magician wants to be serious with his or her insubordination, with the ultimate act of gaining hold, grasp and access, he or she must become an 'alien.' Not the slightest bit of that which once made the magician mortal may be left sticking. The magician finishes things, leading them to their predetermined end; indeed he or she destroys them by finishing them. If the magician was once a materialist, he or she now strives to get to the bottom of concepts such as matter and materialism. What remains? A religion of fear, wounded to death, and a dread of the incalculable and unfathomable. If the magician was once a transcendentalist, he or she now tests religion and mysticism to its limits. Soon these limits are overstretched and what remains is a pitiful pile of misery, the science of managing fear, the dread of the incalculable and unfathomable.

But what about my 'objective' limits? Lucifer the magician may ask. I cannot fly. I have to die. I have to eat and drink. I need warmth. What power inherent to the administration of a reality that has never been closely defined is preventing me from trying? So I'll try, and even be successful. But is that really all there is?

Of course, I can learn astral travel—a substitute for flying, and more than my opponents could ever dream of accomplishing. Of course, I can create a soul that outlives my physical body for as long as I deem fit—a mockery of biological death and a dulling of its sting. Of course, I can learn to fast or modify my physiology like no other mortal could—a disgrace to the science of nutrition. Of course, I can learn Tummo yoga and learn to melt the snow within a ten-foot radius in the iciest of cold environs.

But would that make me physically fly? Could I outlive my physical body by thousands of years or longer? Could I do without eating or drinking for centuries? Could I wander around in the eternal ice without clothes to protect me? What is all my power worth if I contend myself with second-rate skills?

The question itself is put in the wrong manner to begin with, Lucifer the magician realises. Asking questions means setting limits right from the start, striving for acknowledgement in terms of the limits of our 'understanding' (which according to linguistics basically means 'to trample on') where once it was actually freedom that was demanded. On the path to truth we often disremember why we have embarked on this journey in the first place. Not to satisfy our craving (because this would give the adversary the advantage), but, rather, to give it free reign. This forgetting is our final enemy; it's the delusion that denies us access to that which is ours by right of the power and might that we have been striving for and will keep striving for in the future. Our craving must remain insatiable—anything else would be nothing more than conformist whining, asserts Lucifer.

Lucifer realizes: his rebellion is actually not really a rebellion; he shouldn't define himself through his adversaries, nor should he be content with crumbs from the table of the 'Lord.' It is an entirely different, much deeper, far more alien kind of immortality he is striving towards so demandingly and so immodestly. And it will take an immense effort to achieve such a goal because this path is perilous and the henchmen of submission and forgetfulness are lurking everywhere. If they cannot beat the magician, they will attempt to bribe him or her. But the magician is interested in greater things than mere defiance and the crude tricks at slave traders' fairs. The magician wants to be free and merry, abhorring the bullwhip-words 'obligation' and 'must.' There are no limits to the magician's hate, and only through this all-devastating, flaming, boiling hatred concerning the delusion of 'being' that humanity wants to offer up for a gilded cage can the magician become capable of showing love toward those who are truly qualified to call themselves his.

Lucifer the magician proclaims that whoever calls us Satanists is only making a fool of themselves—because we are so much worse, so much more malicious, and so much more corrosive than any Satanist could ever dream to be. Whoever calls us wicked hasn't even an inkling what our darkness is like. Whoever wants to rate us monsters doesn't have the faintest idea how inhuman our being is. Are you searching for our brothers? They are the reptiles. Are you looking for the truth in our eyes? You are staring into eyes as cold as those of a bird of prey. Are you looking for warmth, or maybe even love and affection in us? You will only find them where you partake of our innermost secret: in the true home, in the refuge where nothing alien can prevail and whose cheap, convenient imitation you call a homestead and turn into hell with your sentimentality. Are you looking to reconcile the contradictions? Doesn't the German word for 'reconcile' (*versöhnen*) originally mean to expiate (*versühnen*) i.e. to punish? You won't be able to because they exclude each other. You are not our enemies because that would imply too much of a relationship—instead, you are strangers to us, aliens in the deepest sense of the word. Our kingdom is not of this world, which is why, and only why, we will subjugate the world by rejecting it: living in it, and cauterizing with our poison the very thing that is holy to you; let the jugglery of our sorcery beguile your senses; you will never be able to get hold of us. For our kingdom is not of this world. Lucifer was bitten by the snake. And the snake was he himself. And his name is legion.

And now, in closing, ask yourself:

'Why do I want to become a magician? Wherefore all the effort?'

Casting New Light on Wicca?

THE ROLE OF LUCIFER IN CONTEMPORARY PAGAN WITCHCRAFT

Ethan Doyle White

LUCIFER, THE LORD of Light, is a figure who appears in many guises throughout the vast, heterogenous entity that is the Western esoteric tradition. Aside from Luciferianism, in which Lucifer unsurprisingly represents the central figure of its theistic and mythological structure, this ancient character also appears in various different forms of contemporary religious Satanism, where he is often treated as either a synonym or a facet of Satan. In Thelema, the messianic religious movement founded by Aleister Crowley, Lucifer also makes an appearance, this time as a personification of the emerging Aeon of Horus, a new era for humanity. However, there is a further esoteric religious movement, far larger than the aforementioned three in terms of its number of practitioners, in which Lucifer can also be found: that is the religion of contemporary Pagan Witchcraft, often better known as Wicca.

Lucifer is far from being central to Wicca, and indeed no mention of him is made in many of the core texts associated with the religion. Many practitioners would decry the idea that Lucifer has any part to play in Wiccan theology, assuming him to be one and the same as Satan, the malevolent bogeyman of Christian tradition. Nevertheless, if you look deep enough then you will find him, and in this essay I seek to tease out and explore the appearances that he makes within the tradition. In examining the role of Lucifer in contemporary Pagan Witchcraft, my approach is admittedly not entirely pioneering; instead, it covers some of the ground already articulated by Fredrik Gregorius in his overview of Luciferian Witchcraft, as well as some of my own previous work on the theological structure of the Witchcraft practised by the mid-twentieth century British occultist Robert Cochrane.[1] Nevertheless, rather than simply regurgitating this previously published material, in this essay I seek to take the examination of this evidence into new, unexplored dimensions. In particular, I wish to look at how and why Pagan Witches have legitimised their use of Lucifer as a theological figure by portraying him as a pre-Christian deity who was worshipped by the original 'pagans' of the ancient world.

In the spirit of disclosure, I should specify that I do not identify as a Luciferian, Pagan, or occultist, and that when it comes to the objective, literal existence of preternatural entities such as Lucifer, I remain agnostic. Therefore, the approach that I articulate within this particular paper—and which may well be very different from those of practising Luciferians contributing to this volume—hence focuses on Lucifer as a character and a concept. Whether Lucifer genuinely exists or not is immaterial to this study; what is important is that many people have believed in Lucifer, and have acted in accordance with this belief.[2] However, it should be noted that despite my "outsider" status to the occult traditions that will be discussed, I was born and raised within a cultural and familial context that was replete with esoteric religious movements. Furthermore, for several years I have been actively engaged in the academic field of Pagan studies, over the course of which I have produced historical studies on the early development and emergence of various forms of contemporary Pagan Witchcraft. This essay, produced for a somewhat different audience than that for which I normally write, should therefore be viewed as part of this wider corpus of my work on the subject of Wicca.

1 Fredrik Gregorius, 'Luciferian Witchcraft: At the Crossroads between Paganism and Satanism', pp. 229–49, in Per Faxneld and Jesper Aa. Petersen, eds., *The Devil's Party: Satanism in Modernity*, Oxford University Press, 2013; Ethan Doyle White, 'An Elusive Roebuck: Luciferianism and Paganism in Robert Cochrane's Witchcraft', *Correspondences: An Online Journal for the Academic Study of Western Esotericism* 1, no. 1 (June 2013): pp. 75–101.

2 This approach fits within what in the discipline of religious studies is often termed 'methodological agnosticism.'

PAGAN WITCHCRAFT: THE HISTORICAL BACKGROUND

For the purposes of this essay, I define contemporary Pagan Witchcraft as a new religious movement which emerged from within Britain in the mid twentieth century, initially claiming to be the survival of an ancient pre-Christian witch-cult. Theistically, it typically revolves around the duotheistic veneration of a Horned God and a Goddess (although sometimes branches out into explicitly polytheistic or monotheistic frameworks), and observes a set of seasonal festivals known as Sabbats. Practitioners perform magico-religious rites, either solitarily or in groups known as covens.[3] Even though it is less common for practitioners to claim a direct lineage stretching back into prehistory than it was in past decades, Pagan Witches still typically express a great affinity with the pre-Christian belief systems of Europe, often extending this into a self-perception that the religion constitutes a form of nature-worship. Admittedly, this is a fairly broad-brush definition, but one that I find (from an outsider, academic perspective) to be heuristically very useful, for it allows for the recognition that various magico-religious traditions, such as Gardnerianism, Feri, and Reclaiming Witchcraft, are fundamentally linked as part of a common movement with a shared broad structure and history. At the same time, it is not so broad as to envelop other modern magico-religious movements, such as the Sabbatic Craft or Thelema, into its remit.

Today, the Pagan Witchcraft movement often refers to itself under the term 'Wicca.' Taking as its basis the Old English term for a male sorcerer, *wicca* (pronounced 'witch-uh'), it is a widely held misconception that the term was first developed by Gerald Gardner (1884–1964) in reference to his own tradition of Gardnerian Witchcraft. Instead, Gardner used 'the Wica' (with a singular c) in reference to the community of Pagan Witches as a whole, and it was only in the early 1960s, as Alexandrian Witchcraft came to rise to a level of prominence in the British Craft scene, that 'Wicca' publicly emerged as a term for the religion itself.[4] Thus, as used here, 'Wicca' is essentially a synonym for Pagan Witchcraft, although it must be

3 This is the broad approach that I adopt in Ethan Doyle White, *Wicca: History, Belief, and Community in Modern Pagan Witchcraft*, Sussex Academic Press, 2016.

4 Ethan Doyle White, 'The Meaning of "Wicca": A Study in Etymology, History and Pagan Politics', *The Pomegranate: The International Journal of Pagan Studies* 12, no. 2 (2010): pp. 185–207.

borne in mind that some present day esotericists choose to use it in a more precise manner, to refer explicitly to those traditions of Pagan Witchcraft that make use of the liturgy developed by Gardner, and which can trace a lineaged line of succession back to him.

It is perhaps also necessary to clarify my own definition of contemporary Paganism, or Neo-Paganism, for this essay. Here I use the term in reference to a broad array of modern religious, spiritual, and magical groups which self-consciously adopt elements of the pre-Christian belief systems of Europe, North Africa, and the Near East into their structures. This is not the only definition of the term that exists, however. For some scholars, it has been construed as a singular religion, into which an array of other groups—among them Wicca, Druidry, and Asatru—can be categorised as denominations. However, this is intrinsically problematic, not least because of the sheer diversity among such Neo-Pagan groups. It is more accurate to view these each as singular religions that can be etically categorised under 'contemporary Paganism' as a broad tent family of religions, much as Judaism, Christianity, and Islam come under the broad remit of the 'Abrahamic religion' category.[5]

No religion emerges fully formed from a vacuum. Instead, they typically emerge out of a pre-existing milieu, from which they adopt ideas and concepts; Wicca is no exception. This is an area that has been explored in some depth by a variety of scholars, the most notable of whom is Ronald Hutton, a Professor of History at the University of Bristol.[6] The work of Hutton and others has shown that the early Wiccan pioneers were influenced by a range of factors, from the initiatory degree structure of Freemasonry to the Romanticist depiction of an enchanted natural world. However, one of the central aspects of the milieu from which Wicca emerged was that of prior magical practices, both those of learned, grimoire-reading ceremonial magicians and the folk magicians who plied their trade in their local communities. While some Pagan Witches place great emphasis on the claim that they are the inheritors of the traditions of the rural cunning-

5 I have dealt with this in greater depth in Ethan Doyle White, 'In Defense of Pagan Studies: A Response to Davidsen's Critique', *The Pomegranate: The International Journal of Pagan Studies* 14, no. 1 (2012): pp. 15–17.

6 Ronald Hutton, *The Triumph of the Moon: A History of Modern Pagan Witchcraft*, Oxford University Press, 1999; also examining the esoteric milieu from which Wicca emerged is Joanne Pearson, *Wicca and the Christian Heritage: Ritual, Sex and Magic*, Routledge, 2007 and David Waldron, *The Sign of the Witch: Modernity and the Pagan Revival*, Carolina Academic Press, 2008.

folk, it is nevertheless apparent that the beliefs and typical practices of Wicca are quite dissimilar from those of the wise men and women found in nineteenth and early-twentieth century Britain.[7]

Conversely, it is readily apparent that ceremonial grimoires like *The Key of Solomon* have provided the base outline upon which most Wiccan ritual is built, as can be observed through the use of the ceremonial circle and such ritual tools as the blade, wand, and chalice. In this manner, it has been suggested that Wicca can claim a pedigree that stretches all the way back to the texts of Hellenistic Egypt.[8]

While ceremonial magic gave Wicca an outline for its early magico-religious rites, as a whole the religion owes far more to the witch-cult hypothesis, as articulated by the Egyptologist Margaret Murray (1863–1963). Born in British India, Murray had taken a keen interest in the archaeological study of Ancient Egypt and had studied the subject at University College London, where the department head recognised her value and awarded her a professional position. When the First World War broke out, she was unable to travel to Egypt to continue her excavations, and so turned her attention to a number of issues that were closer to home, among them Arthurian legend and the witch-trial accounts of the early modern period. She developed the idea—albeit one not novel to her—that those accused of witchcraft had been followers of a pre-Christian fertility cult devoted to the veneration of a Horned God whom the Christian persecutors had understood as the Devil.[9] Murray's ideas have not stood the test of time, having been conclusively deconstructed by the in-depth work of historians specialising in the witch trials since the 1960s.[10] Her work was nevertheless

7 See for instance Rae Beth, *Hedgewitch: A Guide to Solitary Witchcraft*, Robert Hale, 1990. The dissimilarity between Wicca and the cunning craft is attested to in Hutton, *The Triumph*, p. 11 and Owen Davies, *Cunning-Folk: Popular Magic in English History*, Hambledon and Continuum, 2003, pp. 195–96, while the interest Pagan Witches have shown in rural cunning-folk is examined in Helen Cornish, 'Cunning Histories: Privileging Narratives in the Present', *History and Anthropology* 16, no. 3 (2005): pp. 363–76.

8 Ronald Hutton, *The Pagan Religions of the Ancient British Isles: Their Nature and Legacy*, Blackwell, 1991, p. 337.

9 A full biography of Murray has recently appeared as Kathleen L. Shepperd, *The Life of Margaret Alice Murray: A Woman's Work in Archaeology*, Lexington, 2013. It devotes comparatively little to her involvement in esoteric matters however, as I point out in Ethan Doyle White, 'Review of Kathleen Shepperd's *The Life of Margaret Alice Murray*', *Aries: Journal for the Study of Western Esotericism* 15, no. 2 (2015): pp. 25–27.

10 Murray's theories had actually faced severe criticism from specialists in the witch trials ever since their first publication, but they would only come to be conclusively refut-

hugely influential, inspiring an array of responses in scholarship, literature, and of course contemporary Paganism, and it is for this reason that she is sometimes thought of as the godmother of Wicca.[11]

It is through Murray that we come to the central theme of this particular essay; Lucifer. In her seminal work, *The Witch-Cult in Western Europe*, published by the prestigious Oxford University Press in 1921, Murray treats Lucifer as a synonym for the Devil, listing him alongside other names for the same entity such as Satan and Beelzebub.[12] Her work is filled with transcripts of actual trial accounts, and a number of those quoted by Murray refer to Lucifer, reflecting the fact that for many early modern Europeans, Lucifer was simply a synonym for the Devil and not a separate entity in his own right.[13] Elsewhere in the book, Murray makes the claim that the practitioners of the ancient witch-cult celebrated 'Sabbaths'—a term that she took from the trial accounts—describing these as the "General Meeting of all members of the religion". She stated that the main Sabbaths were 'May Eve' and 'November Eve', although added that February 2, August 1, Easter, and both solstices were also dates of major religious observance for this witch-cult.[14] As she noted, the Sabbath that fell upon February 2 was often known as 'Candlemas,' and added that on this date, "To call the chief *Lucifer* was therefore peculiarly appropriate" because of his name's

ed by work published in the 1970s. See Norman Cohn, *Europe's Inner Demons: An Inquiry Inspired by the Great Witch-Hunt*, Sussex University Press, 1975, pp. 102–25; Jacqueline Simpson, 'Margaret Murray: Who Believed Her and Why?', *Folklore* 105 no. 1–2 (1994): pp. 89–96; Caroline Oates and Juliette Wood, *A Coven of Scholars: Margaret Murray and her Working Methods*, FLS Books, 1998. Probably the kindest assessment of Murray's theory has been provided by Italian historian Carlo Ginzburg, who opined that there was a "kernel of truth" in her belief that surviving pre-Christian beliefs influenced the early modern witch trials, see Carlo Ginzburg, *The Night Battles: Witchcraft and Agrarian Cults in the Sixteenth and Seventeenth Centuries*, Johns Hopkins Press, 1983, p. xiii.

11 See for instance its use in Helen A. Berger, Evan A. Leach, and Leigh S. Shaffer, *Voices from the Pagan Census: A National Survey of Witches and Neo-Pagans in the United States*, University of South Carolina Press, 2003, p. 9.

12 Margaret Murray, *The Witch-Cult in Western Europe: A Study in Anthropology*, Oxford University Press, 1962 [1921], p. 28.

13 Murray, *The Witch-Cult*, pp. 45, 125.

14 Murray, *The Witch-Cult*, pp. 97, 109. Murray's selection of these dates was dishonest; of the thousands of early modern witch trials accounts, only that of Forfar in 1661 included the claim that the Satanic witches met on the cross-quarter days; see Ronald Hutton, 'Modern Pagan Festivals: A Study in the Nature of Tradition', *Folklore* 119, no. 3 (2008): p. 255.

etymological meaning.[15] She connected this to her belief that fire, in the form of candle-flame, was closely associated with the horned deity of the witch-cult, hence explaining its appearance in a number of trial accounts.

There are two points to note here. The first is that in *The Witch-Cult in Western Europe*, Murray seemingly adopts an understanding of Lucifer from her source material, treating him solely as a synonym for Satan, the Devil. At the same time, she clearly acknowledges the original meaning of his name as 'Light-Bearer.' The second point of interest is that throughout the work she treats the Devil, as he appears in the early modern texts, as the survival of a pre-Christian, pagan fertility deity. When both points are viewed together it becomes apparent that Murray's basic approach allows for the understanding that an entity who was known as Lucifer in early modern Europe was a survival of a pagan god.

While there is evidence to indicate that in her private life Murray was a practitioner of magic,[16] there is no suggestion that she actively attempted to revive the witch-cult which she described in her publications. Nevertheless, there were certainly those who were inspired to do so, and by far the most prominent among them was a man who has come to be known as 'the Father of Wicca', Gerald Gardner (1884–1964). Born to a wealthy middle-class English family, he spent most of his life abroad, working for many years in the Far East. Upon retiring to southern Britain, he settled in the region of the New Forest and involved himself in the local esoteric scene. He later claimed that in 1939 he was initiated into a coven of Pagan Witches, and that it was the tradition which they passed on to him which formed the basis for the Gardnerian tradition which he was publicly propagating by the early 1950s.[17] It remains an issue of contention among scholars of Pagan studies whether this New Forest coven had ever existed at all, with some suggesting that it was instead a fictitious invention of Gardner's to

15 Murray, *The Witch-Cult*, p. 144.

16 Max Mallowan, 'Murray, Margaret Alice (1863–1963),' Oxford Dictionary of National Biography, http://www.oxforddnb.com/index/35/101035169/.

17 The authorised biography of Gardner, which has many traits of autobiography, appeared as Jack Bracelin, *Gerald Gardner: Witch*, Octagon, 1964. It has been superseded by the two-volume study by Philip Heselton, *Witchfather: A Life of Gerald Gardner*, Thoth, 2012, however some reservations regarding the approach in this biography have been expressed in Ethan Doyle White, 'Review of Philip Heselton's *Witchfather: A Life of Gerald Gardner*', *The Pomegranate: The International Journal of Pagan Studies* 14, no. 1 (2012): pp. 171–74.

lend a sense of historical legitimacy to his newly founded faith.[18] Nevertheless, whatever its specific origins, it is clear that Gardner was responsible for shaping his tradition in a manner of his choosing, and that in doing so he drew heavily upon a wide range of older sources.

Alongside his attempts to propagate his Craft among personal acquaintances, Gardner also publicised his faith—which he typically termed 'witchcraft' and "the witch-cult"—through a number of fictional and non-fiction books. It is through studying these publications that we can gain a greater comprehension of how Gardner understood the Craft and its history, and thus is the place where we might expect to find mention of Lucifer. However, Gardner makes very little reference to the Light-Bearer in these works; indeed, there is only a single mention of the name in his first non-fiction book on the subject, *Witchcraft Today* (1954), and none at all in his second, *The Meaning of Witchcraft* (1959). Here, it is not even a direct statement from Gardner himself, but part of a quote from Bishop Wilson, who was reporting a case of witchcraft on the Isle of Man in 1720: "John Curlitt of Murlough, in the county of Down in the parish of Killough, did give himself body and soul to Satan the Devil, who is called Lucifer, after the term of nine years."[19]

This absence is intriguing, for it suggests that Gardner was intentionally avoiding any mention of Lucifer. This was perhaps so as not to provide ammunition for those critics who accused Gardner of practising and promulgating Satanism. Problematising this view is the fact that Gardner makes plenty use of the word 'Devil' and occasional use of 'Satan' in these texts, which were likely to have been just as sinister, if not even more so, in the minds of his detractors. In one passage of *Witchcraft Today* he attempted

18 Heselton presents a compelling, although not conclusive, argument for the existence of the New Forest coven in Philip Heselton, *Wiccan Roots: Gerald Gardner and the Modern Witchcraft Revival*, Capall Bann, 2000 and Philip Heselton, *Gerald Gardner and the Cauldron of Inspiration: An Investigation into the Sources of Gardnerian Witchcraft*, Capall Bann, 2004. He also makes use of this argument in Heselton, *Witchfather*. Two American scholars in particular have suggested it more likely that the coven is a fictitious invention of Gardner's, see Aidan A. Kelly, *Crafting the Art of Magic: A History of Modern Pagan Witchcraft Volume I: 1939–1964*, Llewellyn, 1991, pp. xviii–xix; Aidan A. Kelly, *Inventing Witchcraft: A Case Study in the Creation of a New Religion*, Thoth, 2007, pp. 22–23, 33, 272–73; Chas S. Clifton,'Review of Philip Heselton's *Gerald Gardner and the Cauldron of Inspiration*', *The Pomegranate: The International Journal of Pagan Studies* 6, no. 2 (2004): pp. 5–10; Chas S. Clifton, *Her Hidden Children: The Rise of Wicca and Paganism in America*, AltaMira, 2006, pp. 14–15.

19 Gerald Gardner, *Witchcraft Today*, Rider, 1954, p. 49.

to vindicate himself from any such potential criticism when he noted that "The Devil is, or rather was, an invention of the Church. Witches found that the popular view that Satan was one of them added to their power, and rather adopted it, though they never called him by that name except, perhaps, on the rack."[20] He was insisting that the pagans of the early modern witch-cult never truly called their deity 'Satan' or 'the Devil' unless they were under great duress; so why should he not mention 'Lucifer' here too ?

There is also a second point that should be raised here. There is now growing evidence that Lucifer played a role in many nineteenth-century forms of British folk magic, most notably that of the Society of the Horseman's Word, and that it was this theistic current from which the likes of the Cultus Sabbati have emerged. This growth of Luciferian belief was no doubt influenced by the increased attention that Lucifer was receiving from Romanticist poets like Lord Byron,[21] but also may have something to do with the popularisation of Lucifer as a benevolent bringer of wisdom in the teachings of the Theosophical Society, arguably the most important esoteric organisation of the latter nineteenth century.[22] Had the New Forest coven, from whom Gardner claimed initiation, represented a survival of a nineteenth or early twentieth-century folk magical group, then it may have been expected that they would have inherited a Luciferian theism that Gardner would then have been made aware of. Perhaps this is suggestive of the fact that Gardner's Wicca owed little to the earlier beliefs and practices of nineteenth-century British folk magic, and that the New Forest coven was either fictional or of fairly late emergence. Conversely, it could be that that the coven represented a form of older folk magic which had never embraced a Luciferian world-view, that the coven had expunged these Luciferian elements prior to Gardner's initiation, or that Gardner himself either removed them or sought to hide them from the general reader. As with so many arguments surrounding Wicca's origins, very little can be said conclusively. What can be said for certain is that there is no evidence for any form of clear connection between Gardner's Wicca and earlier forms of Luciferian British folk magic.

20 Gardner, *Witchcraft Today*, p. 132.

21 Lee Morgan, 'The Romantic Age Roots of Witchcraft: Literary and Folk Cross-Pollination in the Nineteenth Century', pp. 331–56, in Michael Howard and Daniel A. Schulke, eds., *Hands of Apostasy: Essays on Traditional Witchcraft*, Three Hands Press, 2014.

22 The Theosophical Society's primary founder and leader, Helena Blavatsky (1831–1891) began issuing an esoteric magazine titled *Lucifer* in 1887, while living in London.

A third, unconnected point worthy of mention is that the work of Murray, and by extension that of Gardner, placed firm emphasis on the idea that the horned Devil who appeared in early modern sources was the survival of a pre-Christian deity. This is an idea that would gain great currency within the Pagan community, and the publications of later Wiccans regularly declare that the Christian iconography of the Devil is based upon that of pre-Christian gods.[23] While Gardner placed no emphasis on Lucifer, and Murray very little, they nevertheless both noted that it was one of the names used for the early modern Devil, and by extension, they both depicted Lucifer as the survival of a pre-Christian deity; this is an idea that we shall see crop up more explicitly in the work of several other Wiccan authors.

CHARLES LELAND, ARADIA, AND ITS RECEPTION IN WICCA:

While it is Murray's theory of the witch-cult that undoubtedly served as the primary influence on the burgeoning Pagan Witchcraft movement's understanding of its own past, a second source has also been identified as being of significant importance. This was a work first published in 1899 titled *Aradia, or the Gospel of the Witches.* The book's author was Charles Godfrey Leland (1824–1903), an American folklorist who spent much of his life in Europe, documenting the beliefs of marginalised groups like the Gypsy community. While in Florence in 1886 he met a young woman whom he referred to as Maddalena, and who—according to his account—claimed to be from a family of practising folk magicians. Hiring her as his research assistant, she provided him with a variety of Tuscan folk charms and stories, on the basis of which he produced two folkloric studies, *Etruscan Roman Remains* (1892) and *Legends of Florence* (1892). Leland claimed that he then heard rumours of a *Vangelo* or witches' gospel, and convinced Maddalena to obtain a copy for him. She duly did so, and Leland went on to publish it alongside much related folkloric material as *Aradia.*[24] The mythology of

23 See for instance Patricia Crowther and Arnold Crowther, *The Witches Speak*, Samuel Weisner, 1976 [1965], p. 7; Stewart Farrar, *What Witches Do: A Modern Coven Revealed*, BCA, 1991 [1971], p. 23; Starhawk, *The Spiral Dance: A Rebirth of the Ancient Religion of the Great Goddess*, Harper SanFrancisco, 1989 [1979], p. 108; Beth, *Hedgewitch*, p. 33.

24 Robert Mathiesen, 'Charles G. Leland and the Witches of Italy: The Origin of Ara-

Aradia revolves around a god and goddess, Diana and her brother Lucifer, who together produce a child, the eponymous Aradia, whom Diana sends to Earth to teach the oppressed peasantry the ways of witchcraft in order that they might defend themselves from the exploitative aristocracy and clergy. In *Aradia*, Lucifer is described as "the god of the Sun and of the Moon, the god of Light (*Splendor*), who was so proud of his beauty, and who for his pride was driven from Paradise."[25] In this manner he is depicted as a pre-Christian deity (or at least, a non-Christian deity associated with facets of the natural world), while at the same time carrying with him some of the Christian mythological associations traditionally applied to the figure.

The context surrounding Leland's *Gospel of the Witches* remains enigmatic. We really don't know if anyone in late nineteenth-century Italy really treated the *Gospel* as a sacred text or whether they genuinely believed in the theistic structure that it espoused. As Hutton has noted, the complete absence of any corroborating evidence for a witch religion devoted to Aradia, Lucifer, and Diana—in an area for which we have strong documentation regarding religious minorities stretching back to the Middle Ages—makes it seem very unlikely that the *Gospel* represents what on face value it claims to be.[26] Instead, it can be suggested that either Maddalena authored the document in the hope of pleasing her employer, or that Leland in part created it himself, perhaps out of a desire to reflect what he thought was the genuine witch religion of past centuries or to provide an outlet for his anti-Catholic beliefs.[27] Whatever its origins, it should be noted that the Gospel undoubtedly draws upon pre-existing folkloric beliefs and characters. Both Diana and Lucifer are mythological figures with a long pedigree in Italian culture, likely as a result of being mentioned in the Bible, while research by folklorist Sabina Magliocco is suggestive of the idea that Aradia was a pre-existing folkloric character found in various parts of Italy, whose name is perhaps a bastardised version of Herodias, another Biblical figure.[28]

dia', pp. 25–57, in Charles G. Leland, eds., *Aradia, or the Gospel of the Witches: A New Translation*, Phoenix Publishing, 1998.

25 Charles Godfrey Leland, 'Aradia, or the Gospel of the Witches', p. 127, in Charles G. Leland, eds., *Aradia, or the Gospel of the Witches: A New Translation*, Phoenix Publishing, 1998.

26 Hutton, *The Triumph*, pp. 145–46.

27 Hutton, *The Triumph*, pp. 146–49.

28 Sabina Magliocco, 'Who Was Aradia? The History and Development of a Legend',

Leland's *Aradia* was published at a time when both anthropology and folkloristics were dominated by a perspective now often known as the 'doctrine of survivals.' Influenced by the new science of geology, this paradigm viewed forms of modern, and in particular rural, folklore as fossilised preservations from the ancient past.[29] In this environment, it would be unsurprising that any nineteenth-century folk character, whether they be Aradia, Diana or Lucifer, would be interpreted as the survival of a pre-Christian deity, something no doubt aided by the knowledge that Diana had indeed once been the name of a Classical goddess.

Although its publication would pre-date the public emergence of Gardnerian Wicca by half a century, the influence of *Aradia* upon early Gardnerianism and other forms of Wicca is blatant.[30] For instance, the idea of holding the Esbats on the full moon is a concept borrowed from *Aradia*, not Murray, while Aradia was chosen as the secret name of the Goddess among the early Gardnerians. Given that this is the case, it is interesting that Lucifer was not chosen as the secret name of the God; instead, the early Gardnerians went for Cernunnos, the suspected name of an antlered deity whose iconography has been found from Iron Age contexts in North-western Europe. Perhaps Gardner chose to avoid Lucifer because he feared its toxic association among the British public (as we have seen, he made next to no mention of Lucifer within his published works on Witchcraft), however the secret name was never meant to made public, so this is perhaps not the likeliest explanation. Instead, it may have been that he felt that Lucifer was simply too satanic a name to use, and that it was fundamentally inappropriate as the name for a horned, pagan god.

While Gardner might not have had much time for Lucifer, his most significant High Priestess—a woman who has come to be known as the "Mother of Modern Witchcraft"—certainly did. This woman was Doreen

The Pomegranate 18 (2001): pp. 5–22; Sabina Magliocco, 'Aradia in Sardinia: The Archaeology of a Folk Character', pp. 40–61, in Dave Evans and Dave Green, eds., *Ten Years of Triumph of the Moon: Academic Approaches to Studying Magic and the Occult*, Hidden Publishing, 2009. Leland himself believed that "Aradia" was an alteration of "Herodias", see Leland, 'Aradia, or the Gospel of the Witches', pp. 225–26.

29 Margaret T. Hodgen, 'The Doctrine of Survivals: The History of an Idea', *American Anthropologist* 33 no. 3 (1931): pp. 307–24; Gillian Bennett, 'Geologists and Folklorists: Cultural Evolution and the Science of Folklore', *Folklore* 105 (1994): pp. 25–37.

30 The impact of Aradia on Pagan Witchcraft is discussed in Chas S. Clifton, 'The Significance of Aradia', pp. 59–77, in Charles G. Leland, eds., *Aradia, or the Gospel of the Witches: A New Translation*, Phoenix Publishing, 1998.

Valiente (1922–1999), and she had developed an interest in occultism through reading books in her local library prior to contacting Gardner and ultimately receiving initiation in 1953. Rising to the position of High Priestess in his Bricket Wood coven, she aided him in rewriting much of the Gardnerian liturgy before splitting with him in 1957 over concerns regarding his incessant publicity seeking. After forming her own coven with fellow Gardnerian defectors, she authored a string of books on various aspects of the Pagan Craft and became a well known figure in the world's Pagan community.[31]

In *An ABC of Witchcraft* (1973), Valiente made reference to Lucifer amidst her wider discussion of Leland's *Aradia*, there referring to him as "the god of the sun."[32] Elsewhere in the book, when discussing the Horned God, she again made reference to Lucifer, asserting that

> *Every year we see re-enacted the Fall of Lucifer, the Light-Bearer, when the sun, the source of vitality for this planet, attains the height of his power at midsummer, and then falls from that height to hide himself in the realms below.*[33]

Although the entity Valiente is describing here is clearly a solar one, she nevertheless tied it in with the Horned God with the statement that the latter represents "the power of returning vitality in the spring."[34] Valiente was an individual with a clear interest in the historical development of the Lucifer character; under her entry on demonology in the book, she comments that "The identification of Satan with Lucifer rests upon a text in Isaiah," before proceeding to provide a brief outline of how she believed the two entities had come to be conflated, before adding her own moral judgment of the situation: "Out of such doubtful beginnings did religious doctrines grow, with the assistance of pious and semi-literate demonologists."[35] Thus, we can see that Valiente herself was clearly critical of the conflation of Lucifer with Satan, instead being sympathetic to

31 Valiente provides an overview of her life in Doreen Valiente, *The Rebirth of Witchcraft*, Robert Hale, 1989, although a short biography has also been made available as Jonathan Tapsell, *Ameth: The Life and Times of Doreen Valiente*, Avalonia, 2013.

32 Doreen Valiente, *An ABC of Witchcraft: Past and Present*, Robert Hale, 1986 [1973], p. 14.

33 Valiente, *An ABC of Witchcraft*, pp. 182–83.

34 Valiente, *An ABC of Witchcraft*, p. 182.

35 Valiente, *An ABC of Witchcraft*, pp. 81–82.

the idea of viewing them as separate and distinct entities, the former of which was a non-Christian deity. In her own largely autobiographical account of Wiccan history, *The Rebirth of Witchcraft* (1989), she discussed Leland's *Aradia* in her second chapter before stating that:

> *The word Lucifer is simply Latin for 'light-bearer.' Yet it has evidently become confused with the Christian idea of Satan, represented as a rebel archangel who fell from Heaven. This concept is, I think, something that has been grafted on to a much older story. 'The god of the old religion is the devil of the new.' The Christian Devil, with his horns, hoofs and tail, is simply another version of the great and ancient god Pan, who in his turn was derived distantly from the old Horned God of the painted caves. He is the male element in nature, the principle of fire, the sun and the phallus.*[36]

Several pages later, Lucifer is mentioned again. Here, Valiente expressed the view that his name may be connected to the Sanskrit term *Deva*, which she translated as "a shining one, a god" and claimed to be cognate with the Latin *Deus*.[37] Privately, Valiente was willing to go further; in a 1977 letter to Michael Howard she stated that she had no problem with Lucifer being used as the "name for the old god," while in a 1998 letter she went on to express her belief that Lucifer was in fact "the true name of the god of the Old Religion".[38] This is not a view that she publicly espoused in her books, likely out of fear of the negative attention which it would generate both within the Wiccan community and from outside of it.

Valiente was not the only prominent Wiccan to have gained her understanding of Lucifer from Leland's text. A similar interpretation appears in the lectures of Alex Sanders (1926–1988), an Englishman who had been initiated into the Gardnerian tradition in 1963 before using it as a basis upon which to develop his own Alexandrian tradition of Wicca, which he then passed off as an old hereditary tradition, claiming that it had been inherited from his grandmother.[39] In his lectures, which would be published as a small, collected volume in 1984, Sanders provided an account

36 Doreen Valiente, *The Rebirth of Witchcraft*, Robert Hale, 1989, p. 22.

37 Valiente, *Rebirth of Witchcraft*, p. 26.

38 Michael Howard, *Modern Wicca: A History from Gerald Gardner to the Present*, Llewellyn, 2009, p. 271.

39 For a biography of Sanders, see Jimahl di Fiosa, *A Coin for the Ferryman: The Death and Life of Alex Sanders*, Logios, 2010, as well as the autobiography of his wife, Maxine Sanders, *Firechild: The Life and Magic of Maxine Sanders, 'Witch Queen'*, Mandrake, 2008.

of the Diana and Lucifer myth, as originally found within *Aradia*, but followed this with a discussion of the Descent of the Goddess, a myth which appears in Gardnerian Wicca, and it is here that he refers to "Lucifer, the Horned God."[40] This is significant, for it is one of the few instances where Lucifer is specifically used as the name of the Horned God, the central male deity within Wiccan theology, rather than being used in reference to an explicitly solar deity. Elsewhere in the lectures, Sanders stated that the name of the Wiccan God was "a closely-guarded secret" but that historically, Christians had termed him the Devil, Satan, Beelzebub, and "Lucifer (more correctly *Lucifuge*—The Light-Bringer")."[41]

Two of Sanders' most prominent initiates, Stewart Farrar (1916–2000) and his wife Janet Farrar (b.1950), also quoted Leland's work on Lucifer in their book on *The Witches' God* (1989), in which they sought to identify many different facets of the male Wiccan divinity. They identified Leland's Lucifer as "the Son/Lover God", an entity who both mated with, and was born from, the Goddess.[42] In discussing this form of deity, they proceeded to claim that "this pattern—of the primordial, uncreated Mother giving birth to all things, including her own male counterpart...is the earliest foundation of all mythology and all religion."[43] However, later in the book they took a different interpretation of the deity when discussing "the Anti-God", an entity reflecting the forces of destruction and darkness. Here, they made reference to Lucifer but treated him simply as a synonym of Satan, thus accepting the traditional Christian understanding of the entity that was dominant at the time.[44]

A further source in which the influence of Leland's Lucifer is apparent is *Mastering Witchcraft: A Practical Guide for Witches, Warlocks & Covens*, authored by Paul Huson (b. 1942) and published in 1970.[45] The first book to be released that explained to the reader how to become a Pagan Witch or Wiccan in a step-by-step manner, *Mastering Witchcraft* would soon be

40 Alex Sanders, *The Alex Sanders Lectures*, Magickal Childe, 1984, pp. 71–76.

41 Sanders, *Alex Sanders Lectures*, p. 9.

42 Stewart Farrar and Janet Farrar, *The Witches' God: Lord of the Dance*, Robert Hale, 1989, p. 7.

43 Farrar and Farrar, *Witches' God*, p. 8.

44 Farrar and Farrar, *Witches' God*, pp. 54–55.

45 Some will take issue with my description of *Mastering Witchcraft* as a "Wiccan" book; it has indeed been referred to as "non-Wiccan" in Gregorius, 'Luciferian Witchcraft', p. 239. However, the structure of the magico-religious tradition it espouses easily fits within the wider rubric of Pagan Witchcraft as it is used here.

followed by an array of similar offerings, from Raymond Buckland's *The Tree* (1974) to Silver RavenWolf's *To Ride a Silver Broomstick* (1994). Huson's work nevertheless remained distinct, and this was in large part due to the unique theological structure that it espoused. In keeping with the ideas of many Wiccans, Huson drew his Lucifer from Leland's *Aradia*, describing the Lucifer-Diana story and attributing it to "Italian witch lore" rather than specifying its peculiarly Tuscan origin. He then added the observation that the story had "gnostic overtones" akin to the Kabbalistic story of Naamah and Azael, and intriguingly referred to Lucifer as Diana's "alter ego."[46] Several pages on, he stated that both Lucifer and Diana were "but figurative forms" of "the Watchers, the Mighty Ones of the Heavenly Places, the parents of giant and human alike as seen in symbolic and archetypal form as the parents of humanity", whose existence he believed were attested to in various ancient mythologies and in texts like the Zohar.[47] Much later in *Mastering Witchcraft*, Huson included Lucifer in his list of names for the Magister, adding that the name refers to the god "seen as the spirit of light and, hence, the sun."[48]

Leland's conception of the entity was also adopted by maverick archaeologist T. C. Lethbridge (1901–1971) in his 1962 book *Witches: Investigating an Ancient Religion*. Although there is no evidence to suggest that Lethbridge himself was a practitioner of Wicca, he was nonetheless deeply interested in paranormal phenomena, and was an early pioneer of what came to be known as the Earth Mysteries movement. Inspired by the publication of both Gardner's books and those of Murray—a woman he described as "an old friend"[49]—he devoted the book to what he saw as an exploration of the ancient origins of the witch-cult, in doing so drawing haphazardly from a multitude of archaeological, historical, and folkloric sources. In the book he turned to Leland's *Aradia*, suggesting that its references to a tyrannical clergy date it to around the fourteenth century; he subsequently referred to Lucifer and Diana as the witch-cult's deities, thus transposing them across Europe and throughout the centuries.[50] Furthermore, he described the alleged prehistoric hill figures on Wandlebury Hill, Cam-

46 Paul Huson, *Mastering Witchcraft: A Practical Guide for Witches, Warlocks & Covens*, Putnam, 1970, p. 11.

47 Huson, *Mastering Witchcraft*, p. 14.

48 Huson, *Mastering Witchcraft*, p. 214.

49 T.C. Lethbridge, *Witches: Investigating an Ancient Religion*, Routledge and Kegan Paul, 1962, p. 41.

50 Lethbridge, *Witches*, pp. 7, 17.

bridgeshire as "Lucifer and Diana...in very primitive guise."[51] However, unlike the aforementioned approach of Sanders, who conflated the figures of Lucifer and the Horned God, Lethbridge viewed them separately, treating Lucifer as a solar deity and suggesting that Diana had taken both Lucifer and Pan, the horned god, as her lover.[52]

The influence of Leland's *Aradia* is also apparent in one of the brief articles authored by the enigmatic English occultist E. W. 'Bill' Liddell, who achieved notability in the 1970s for his highly controversial claims regarding the Essex cunning man George Pickingill (c.1816–1909).[53] Liddell claimed that his contacts with various covens, cunning lodges, and his family's own hereditary tradition gave him important insights into both Pickingill and into the history of witchcraft more generally. Problematically, Liddell's claims are regularly self-contradictory, far-fetched, and at odds with scholarly interpretations of the history of witchcraft; as accurate accounts of past events they are fundamentally inappropriate. They nevertheless offer useful insights into how some Crafters in the latter part of the twentieth century were interpreting and articulating the histories of their own religion. The 1970s had witnessed the thorough rejection of the Murrayite hypothesis within academia, as scholars like Keith Thomas and Norman Cohn performed more extensive research into the witch trial documents themselves. To some extent this rubbed off on the Pagan community; the American Pagan journalist Margot Adler (1946–2014) suggested that most Wiccans in the U.S. had recognised the flaws of the Murrayite approach by 1975.[54] These new understandings of the history of witchcraft left the traditional Wiccan origin myth in a highly precarious position, as it became clear that Wicca was not the genuine survival of an ancient pre-Christian faith. To avoid the appearance that Wicca was simply a new religious movement with no historical roots, many practitioners began to look elsewhere for their historical pedigree, including to forms of nineteenth and early twentieth-century folk magic which pre-dated the public emergence of Wicca.

51 Lethbridge, *Witches*, p. 92.

52 Lethbridge, *Witches*, p. 66.

53 For an excellent overview of Pickingill's life, as it can be ascertained from reliable historical sources, see the work of independent scholar William Wallworth, 'George Pickingill', Deadfamilies.com, 2012, http://www.deadfamilies.com/Z3-Others/Pickingill/George-Pickingill.htm.

54 Margot Adler, *Drawing Down the Moon: Witches, Druids, Goddess-Worshippers and Other Pagans in America*, third edition, Penguin, 2006, p. 83.

Liddell's publications must be seen as part of this growing trend; in his early letters, he had seemingly adopted the Murrayite hypothesis of a surviving pre-Christian religion, referring to the Pickingill family as having been priests of a pagan religion devoted to the Horned God since the eleventh century.[55] Several years later, he had changed his approach, claiming that the witch-cult was not a pagan survival after all, but that it had developed in fifteenth-century France through a union of Christian heretics, cunning lodges, and Luciferians.[56] In doing so, he stated that a sense of camaraderie developed between members of the witch-cult and Freemasonry, because both owed a "common allegiance to Lucifer, the Lightbearer." Illustrating a probable influence from Leland, he then went on to refer to both Lucifer and Diana as entities that had been present in Britain from at least the early modern.[57] It is noteworthy that his latter articles appeared in *The Cauldron*, a British esoteric magazine whose founder and editor, Michael Howard, developed the term "Luciferian Craft"—from which "Luciferian Witchcraft" has been extrapolated—as a term with which to describe Witchcraft groups whose theistic beliefs revolve around Lucifer.[58]

Leland's *Aradia* is an interesting and important text in part because it clearly intersects both the categories of Pagan Witchcraft and Luciferian Witchcraft, and in doing so blurs the boundaries that exist between them. As a seminal text in the early development of Pagan Witchcraft, there can be no doubt that many of the faith's early pioneers were well aware of its concept of Lucifer as a solar deity of the Witches. Thus, they were then in the position to make an active choice as to whether to adopt him into their own traditions or not. In the case of Gardner, it seems apparent that he actively avoided doing so, although for a number of others—most notably Doreen Valiente but also Alex Sanders and the sympathetic outsider T. C. Lethbridge—Lucifer remained an enigmatic figure worthy of mention, both as sun god and horned god.

55 E.W. Liddell, *The Pickingill Papers: George Pickingill and the Origins of Modern Wicca*, Capall Bann, 1994, p. 25.

56 Hutton, *The Triumph*, p. 291.

57 Liddell, *Pickingill Papers*, pp. 75–77.

58 Michael Howard, pers. comm., 06/25/2012. The term 'Luciferian' itself is older, having been used by the Medieval Inquisition in reference to certain heretics, see Gareth J. Medway, *Lure of the Sinister: The Unnatural History of Satanism*, New York University Press, 2001, p. 12.

LUCIFER AS AN ANCIENT PAGAN DEITY

Although he did not outright declare that Lucifer had once been a pre-Christian deity, Leland's ideas had clearly emerged from an intellectual milieu dominated by the folkloric doctrine of survivalism, and he did suggest that the traditions included in the Gospel had ancient Etruscan or Latin origins.[59] From there, it would only be a very small step to the view that the characters who feature in the Gospel—Aradia, Diana, and of course Lucifer—themselves might have ancient origins. Given this milieu, it was unsurprising that Murray and Gardner believed that the horned deity of the early modern witch-cult—who was sometimes named Lucifer in the trial accounts—was the survival of an ancient god. There was thus plenty of basis from which the idea of Lucifer as an ancient pagan god could grow within the Pagan Witchcraft movement, and that is precisely what happened. In his aforementioned tome, *Witches*, Lethbridge expressed the view that:

> *Lucifer the light-bearer figures in the witch trials and is alternatively known as Beelzebub, or the Devil. Lucifer was known over much of Gaul, Britain and Ireland as Lugh (the Latin: Lux). Places like Lyons in France still bear his name, for Lyons was once Lugudunum, Lugh's dun, or fort. Lugh's name still survives in Britain today. There is a Lugmoor on the hill just above the house where I am writing this.*[60]

Lethbridge subsequently emphasised that "Lucifer and the sun are synonymous", adding that "In Roman terms Lucifer is Apollo. In the Welsh lands Apollo was Mabon (or Maponus). Beelzebub, known to the Celts as Bel, Beli, Balor and so on, who burnt people up with his fiery glance, is only another name for Lucifer or Lugh."[61] With this dubious use of argument, Lethbridge equated Lucifer with a range of other pre-Christian mythological figures from various parts of Europe. He proceeded to look at the process of Christianisation with the statement that "Lugh apparently

59 Leland, 'Aradia, or the Gospel of the Witches', p. 239.

60 Lethbridge, *Witches*, pp. 45–6. "Lugh" is a figure from Medieval Irish mythology, and various scholars suggested that this was a survival of a putative solar or fire deity that could be found in many linguistically Celtic societies of Iron Age Europe. It is this deity to whom Lethbridge refers.

61 Lethbridge, *Witches*, p. 46.

became Michael and Mabon became Andrew", both of whom were Christian saints.[62] Lethbridge's perceived links between Lucifer and Lugh here would be cited by the Farrars in their book, *Eight Sabbats for Witches* (1981). Basing their approach on the idea of pagan survivals, they added that the figure of St. Michael was "a later form" of Lucifer, and that the festival of Michaelmas was thus "the festival of Michael/Lucifer, Archangel of Fire and Light."[63] Other Wiccans would also embrace the idea that Lucifer had his origins as a pre-Christian deity, but would take it in new directions. For instance, Zsuzsanna Budapest (b. 1940), the Hungarian-American founder of the feminist-oriented tradition of Dianic Wicca, declared that Lucifer represented a Christian demonisation of an ancient "sun goddess", Lucina.[64]

Contemporary Pagan Witches are not the only ones to have specifically portrayed Lucifer as a pre-Christian deity. Anton LaVey (1930–1997), the American founder of LaVeyan Satanism—an atheistic magico-religious movement which venerates Satan as a personification of human nature—made reference to the idea in his seminal 1969 text, *The Satanic Bible*. Here, he stated that

> *The Roman god, Lucifer, was the bearer of light, the spirit of the air, the personification of enlightenment. In Christian mythology he became synonymous with evil.*[65]

Given that LaVey was known to appropriate much of his information from earlier sources,[66] it might be suggested that this idea of Lucifer as a Roman god was an earlier one which he adopted.

The depiction of Lucifer as a pre-Christian deity is also very much present in a number of recent Luciferian publications. In their exposition of Luciferian religion, Nigel Jackson and Michael Howard described "the firstborn emanations from the Divine Mind" as angelic entities whose ex-

62 Lethbridge, *Witches*, p. 47.

63 Stewart Farrar and Janet Farrar, *Eight Sabbats for Witches*, Robert Hale, 1981, pp. 105, 116.

64 Zsuzsanna Budapest, *The Holy Book of Women's Mysteries: Volume I* (revised ed.), Susan B. Anthony Coven No. 1, 1986, p. 143.

65 Anton LaVey, *The Satanic Bible*, Avon Books, 1969, p. 39.

66 Eugene V. Gallagher, 'Sources, Sects, and Scripture: *The Book of Satan* in The Satanic Bible', pp. 103–22, in Per Faxneld and Jesper Aa. Petersen, eds., *The Devil's Party: Satanism in Modernity*, Oxford University Press, 2013.

istence had been acknowledged by ancient pre-Christian societies such as ancient Egypt; for instance, they identified the Egyptian god Osiris as an avatar of the angel Lucifer.[67] Another publicly prominent Luciferian Witch, Shani Oates (b. 1959), also portrayed Lucifer as one of a number of "angelic beings", whom she termed the "Great Higher Council of Seven", and whose existence—she believed—had been recorded in a number of ancient mythologies.[68] Oates is the Magistra of an English occult group known as the Clan of Tubal Cain, which she states is based upon a Luciferian and Gnostic mythos. However, there is also a rival Clan of Tubal Cain operating in California whose leaders, Dave and Ann Finnin, instead describe their practices as Pagan. Both groups trace their lineage via Evan John Jones (1936–2003) back to the highly influential English Witch Roy Bowers, who was better known under his pseudonym of Robert Cochrane (1931–1966).

Cochrane rose to notability as the leader of a Witches' group known as the Thames Valley Coven, around whom revolved the wider Clan of Tubal Cain, a sort of occult family. Born to a working-class family in West London, he later claimed to have been instructed in his family's Witchcraft tradition, although this has been refuted by both his widow and relatives. Instead, it appears that Cochrane only embarked on his study of the esoteric after attending a talk given by the Society for Psychical Research in Kensington.[69] Establishing his coven circa 1961 along with his wife Jane and friends George Stannard (c. 1912–1983) and Ronald White (1928–1998), the group remained active until 1966, during which time they attracted new members, among them Valiente, who by this time had separated from Gardner's tradition.[70] Although he achieved wider influence through a number of important articles and correspondences, personal problems led Cochrane to undertake a suicidal ritual at Midsummer 1966, resulting in his death several days later.[71] Today, he is widely cited as an inspiration by

67 Nigel Jackson and Michael Howard, *The Pillars of Tubal-Cain*, Capall Bann, 2000, pp. 6–8.

68 Shani Oates, *Tubelo's Green Fire: Mythos, Ethos, Female, Male and Priestly Mysteries of the Clan of Tubal Cain*, Mandrake, 2010, pp. 15–17.

69 Michael Howard, *Children of Cain: A Study of Modern Traditional Witches*, Three Hands Press, 2011, pp. 41–43.

70 Gillian Spraggs with Shani Oates, *Genuine Witchcraft is Explained: The Secret History of the Royal Windsor Coven and the Regency*, Capall Bann, 2011; Howard, *Children of Cain*, p. 43.

71 Gavin Semple, *The Poisoned Chalice: The Death of Robert Cochrane*, Reineke Verlag,

practising Witches across the world, becoming an almost totemic figure for many of those who identify as 'Traditional Witches.'

Oates' reference to seven angelic beings has parallels in a document allegedly authored by Cochrane as part of his correspondence with the English Witch Norman Gills. Titled "The Basic Structure of the Craft", in this text he referred to 'Lucet' as being one of the seven children of the Gods, stating that:

> *Lucet is the King of Light, Fire, Love and Intellect, of Birth and Joy... the Child. He is visualised as a bright golden light moving quickly with wings. Thieving and mischievous. Sometimes he comes as a tall golden man, moving rapidly, other times the wings of Fire surround him, but few can face the vision without aid from an even Higher Source. At time he is winged at the foot; at others upon the head, behind the glorious hair.*[72]

In another, undated letter to Gills, Cochrane refers to this entity more specifically as Lucifer, describing him as "the Angel of Light" who appears as a "tall golden man, moving rapidly" and who is sometimes seen with "wings of fire." However, he warned that "few can face that vision without aid from an even Higher Source."[73] In his correspondences, Cochrane listed three other children of the Gods as Tettens, Carenos and Node, the latter two of which are most probably bastardised names of the Iron Age deities Cernunnos and Nodens;[74] in this way, Cochrane's theistic structure situated Lucifer alongside the names of pre-Christian deities, leading to the possibility that he too may have deemed Lucifer to have once been a pagan god.

What therefore are we to make of this appearance? While there is clearly a character, known as Lucifer or Lucet, who appears within Cochrane's theistic system, he is far from a central figure, being simply one among seven other entities identified as the spawn of the Gods, several of whom are clearly named after ancient deities. These angelic entities were subordi-

2004.

72 Robert Cochrane, letter to Norman Gills, undated, reproduced in Cochrane with Jones and Howard, *Robert Cochrane Letters*, p. 164.

73 Robert Cochrane, letter to Norman Gills, undated, reproduced in Robert Cochrane with Evan John Jones and Michael Howard, *The Robert Cochrane Letters: An Insight into Modern Traditional Witchcraft*, Capall Bann, 2002, p. 157.

74 Robert Cochrane, letter to Norman Gills, undated, reproduced in Cochrane with Jones and Howard, *Robert Cochrane Letters*, pp. 164–66.

nate to a number of higher beings, including a Goddess—at least once referred to as Diana in a possible influence from Leland's *Aradia*—a God, and a Horn Child, all of which were identified as manifestations of a greater Godhead. Ultimately, an analysis of both the available textual evidence and the testimony of those who personally knew and worked with Cochrane paints a picture of a man who had developed his own form of contemporary Pagan Witchcraft, not dissimilar in many ways from Gardnerianism and other traditions which had appeared at this time.[75] It is noteworthy, perhaps, that an argument has been presented that Cochrane was possibly initiated into a Gardnerian coven that was based in West London.[76]

Most contemporary Pagan religions place great emphasis on their perceived links with the pre-Christian, "pagan" religions of the ancient world, arguing for a sense of continuity, either in the form of a direct line of succession (as with, for instance, Wiccan use of the Murrayite witch-cult) or through the argument that the gods which they are worshipping are also those worshipped by the ancients. This being the case, in those instances where Pagan Witches incorporate Lucifer into their mythos, it would be unsurprising that they interpreted him as a manifestation or survival of a pagan god, whether Roman or "Celtic"; in doing so, they legitimate their perceived links to the ancient past and avoid many of the claims that they are venerating a Satanic deity. It is interesting that both Luciferians and Satanists have similarly purported the idea of Lucifer being some sort of pre-Christian deity, although perhaps for very different reasons. Luciferians identify angelic beings such as Lucifer as entities with an objective existence who have aided the development of humanity; from this perspective it would be evident that the ancient pagan gods may have been reflections of this angelic-human interaction. Conversely, in the case of LaVey, it is his staunch anti-Christian attitude that may have led to him adopting the view that Christianity had simply stolen the idea and name

75 Doyle White, 'Elusive Roebuck'.

76 Ethan Doyle White, 'Robert Cochrane and the Gardnerian Craft: Feuds, Secrets, and Mysteries in Contemporary British Witchcraft', *The Pomegranate: The International Journal of Pagan Studies* 13, no. 2 (2011): pp. 33–52. While originally articulating this argument, further contemplation of this issue has resulted in me concluding that an alternative scenario is equally if not more likely—that in the late 1950s Cochrane was a member of a non-Gardnerian coven in West London, many of whose members (including 'Taliesin') later became Gardnerian. Cochrane therefore learned more about the tradition without himself being initiated.

of Lucifer from earlier sources, thus painting Christianity in a somewhat negative light.

CONCLUDING THOUGHTS

Even a quick Google search reveals that the role of Lucifer within Wicca is one that attracts interest.[77] Nevertheless, many Wiccans still express concern and opposition to Lucifer and Luciferianism, either because they associate it with malevolent magic and Satanism or because they fear that the general public will do so, resulting in negative consequences for Wiccans themselves.[78] Conversely, others have taken a different view. Most notable perhaps was the prominent English non-Gardnerian Wiccan Alastair "Bob" Clay-Egerton (1930–1998), who practised both magico-religious traditions, although believed that there were "some basic differences between those Wiccans and pagans who are Luciferian and those who are not."[79] What this essay has established is that while many Wiccans will be uncomfortable with the idea, Lucifer nevertheless makes appearances in their religion. While he is far from being a major figure within Wiccan theism, he reappears on a number of occasions throughout the literature of several key figures within the Wiccan movement, who have interpreted him in various different ways.

Many in the Wiccan movement—such as Gerald Gardner himself—apparently made no public differentiation between the figures of Lucifer and Satan, treating them simply as synonyms, much as most folk in Christendom had done for many centuries. This approach was one inherited from the "Godmother of Wicca", Margaret Murray, and led to Lucifer being rejected as a Wiccan deity, likely in an attempt to remove any overtly Satanic elements from what was being promulgated as the survival of an ancient pagan religion. However, a very different approach also emerged in early

77 "Lucifer?", Wiccan Together, http://www.wiccantogether.com/forum/topics/1070680:Topic:552599.

78 The very real opposition and persecution that Wiccans face is explored in Catharine Cookson, 'Reports from the Trenches: A Case Study of Religious Freedom Issues Faced by Wiccans Practicing in the United States', *Journal of Church and State* 39, no. 4 (1997): pp. 723-48 and Carol Barner-Barry, *Contemporary Paganism: Minority Religions in a Majoritarian America*, Palgrave Macmillan, 2005.

79 A. R. Clay-Egerton, *Coven of the Scales: The Collected Writings of Bob Clay-Egerton*, Ignotus, 2002, p. 105.

Wicca, rooted in the fact that Lucifer was a common figure in various forms of European esotericism, folk magic, and folklore, where his identity was established as being distinct from that of Satan. Lucifer's appearance as a solar god of the witches in Leland's *Aradia* was something that exerted a clear impact on key Wiccan thinkers like Doreen Valiente, Alex Sanders, and Stewart and Janet Farrar, for some of whom he was a solar deity and for others a name of the horned god himself. Wicca's great emphasis on the pre-Christian past led an array of practitioners to express the view that Lucifer had once been a deity in ancient Europe, an idea also expressed by prominent Luciferians and Satanists. In this way, bridges were erected between the contemporary Pagan and Luciferian traditions of Witchcraft, potentially having far reaching effects for the future of these two magico-religious movements.

The Hidden Stone

DEVOTION, LUCIFER AND THE HIGH SABBAT

Robert Fitzgerald

(for the Two Brothers)

CURSORY EXAMINATION OF Continental and American witchcraft trial records shows the repeated use of the names Satan and Lucifer, used both by inquisitor and accused alike. In-depth study reveals their essential conflation, an admixture of identities that continues to the present day within modern occult writings. While erroneous in essence (given their very different origins and characters), both Satan and Lucifer have also served as the Man-in-Black of the Sabbat, the presiding Master of the Grand Rite of the Witches. More so Lucifer, who was adopted by European witches as far flung as from Italy to Scotland beginning in the 13th century.[1]

The magical function and office of Lucifer in early witchcraft groups and individuals was dual, in the sense that he was both Light-Bringer or Illuminator who bore the Torch of Wisdom upon his brow, and also, the Black Man, or Devil who led the sabbats of the covine. This function ob-

1 Charles G. Leland. Aradia, or *The Gospel of the Witches. A New Translation* trans. Mario and Dina Pazzaglini. Phoenix Publishing. Blaine, Washington, 1998. Lawrence Normand and Gareth Roberts. *Witchcraft in Early Modern Scotland.* University of Exeter Press. Exeter, UK. 2000.

tains today within some occult groups one could rightly call 'Luciferian' in nature and worship.

One witchcraft sodality operant in modern times is the Cultus Sabbati, which originated from several lineal streams hailing from Wales and Essex. The primary patterning of belief and ritual practice within this group is the Witches' Sabbat. Within the Cultus exist specific cells or magical groups unavowedly Luciferian in nature, and although many of these historical Luciferic strands of lore and practice in the Cultus remain of inner provenance, and are thereby hidden, some are visible in the public eye and demonstrate the Illuminist metaphysic of the Cult. Of these, perhaps the most succinct and well known is a ritual rubric by Andrew D. Chumbley, 'A Lover's Call to the Angel of Witchblood,' subtitled, 'A Transvocation of Az'Ra-Lumial.' While there exist various recensions of this ritual practice, each completed at different points in time, the one which is appended to this article is the most complete version, first published in Michael Howard's *The Book of Fallen Angels.*[2]

The purpose of this paper is to present to the public an extended commentary on this very specialized practice in the hopes that its Luciferian anatomy may be clearly elucidated, and that the true function of the rite is explained, dissipating some of the gross and fatuous misunderstandings that have accrued around it in the intervening years since it first saw publication.

The ritual itself was composed by Andrew Chumbley in the summer of 2003 for dissemination to the general public. It is a specialized recension of the ritual praxis known as 'Hallowing the Kingdom of Q̤ayin': a circle-casting rite of which Chumbley wrote:

> *In essence the Circle is the all-encompassing Sphere of Magical Power cast outward from the inmost point of one's Being to form a numinous horizon—an orb of æthyric light—about one's physical, mental and spiritual body. Its intent is to purify, to protect, to consecrate one's immediate sphere of existence—to literally 'hallow the kingdom' of the Seeker: the Magically Self-existant One.*[3]

The 'Hallowing' praxis originates in Chumbley's *The Dragon Book of Essex*, and constellates the powers of the Dragon or Elder Serpent about the

2 Michael Howard, *The Book of Fallen Angels* (Capall Bann, 2003).

3 Chumbley, *The Dragon Book of Essex* (San Franscisco: Xoanon 2014), 804.

practitioner in the form of Qayin (Cain), considered within the lore of the Cultus as the first sorcerer and an ancestor of witches.[4] Once transformed into the 'Transvocation' however, the Hallowing rite takes on several other functions, of which the following commentary shall serve to clarify, especially in regards to the Luciferian nature of the entity Az'Ra-Lumial.

The rite is divided into four parts. The first of these is the Petition of the power to be summoned, namely Az'Ra-Lumial. Who is this entity? The answer is given through the process of exacting the rite itself, a progressive unveiling of identity through gradual illumination.

The practitioner first offers himself to the ritual, and to its present moment of exaction. As in all Draconian rites and practices, it is the practitioner who must stand in the various Circles of Art and embody the spirit of Cain, the First Initiator. This is hinted at by the calling upon the Lightning Bolt, the Flaming Torch and the Serpent's Fire in the first paragraph of the rite. These three are the attributes or powers that reside in the Tridentate Staff of Azha-Cain, the initiating aspect of Cain, patron of witches. It is they who bring strength, force and wisdom to the ritual, and they emanate from within the Initiated Body of the practitioner.

This is one of the deeper mysteries of the Draconist Temple within Cultus Sabbati, that Cain must be enfleshed within the Circle, and within each Initiate who speaks his 'liturgy': the Rites of the Serpent's Brood.

In the second paragraph of the rite, the identity of Az'Ra-Lumial is first defined. He is the literal 'Angelick Soul of the Master Cain.' Lumial is the bringer of the Light of Gnosis, and the Solely Manifest One of the Elder Gods within the Cosmogony and Theurgy of the Cult. As such he is an hypostasis of Lucifer, also of angelic derivation. This 'Angelick Soul' informs and imbibes the Crooked Path in its entirety, from solitary to Draconick manifestations. The practitioner calls him thus, and opens his heart to him as a 'vessel'. This is a direct reference to the ritualized manner through which the Draconic rites are performed: via the instruments of the Marriage and Phoenix vessels, both enlivened by the spirit of Azha-Cain, amongst others. In this rite, one opens one's heart to the Angel of Light.

The Vessel has long been a votive and sacramental tool of witch and sorcerer, especially within the Sabbatic Cultus. In the work of the Dragon-rites, two primary vessels are utilized. The first, called the Marriage Vessel, serves as the repository of *numina* for the inception Rite of Ka, in which

4 Daniel Schulke, 'Cainite Gnosis and the Sabbatic Tradition', *The Cauldron* 143, 2012.

the practitioner unites himself with the Stellar Dragon Azhdeha for an entire dark moon cycle prior to Winter Solstice. In this act he enfleshes the Draconic power as Cain Azha-Ka, who embodies the ever-living spirit of Azra'Lumial. The second, called the Phoenix Vessel, serves as a spectral link to the form of Azha-Cain in his guise of the Peacock Angel, who in turn is a hypostate of Azra'Lumial during the Rite of Ra, undertaken at Summer Solstice. These twin vessels are thus physical foci for both stellar and chthonic manifestations of Luciferian Gnosis.

In the next phase of the Transvocation, the practitioner places his step in the Void Place of Spirit, or the 'Empty Circle of the Royal Arte.' This is an arcanum belonging to the inner orders of Cultus Sabbati. The Empty Circle is a reference to the Third Circle Arena of the *Auræon*, a late work by Chumbley dealing with the higher metaphysics of Sabbatic Craft.

In the gnostic cosmology of the Sabbatic Tradition there is the Void and the Elder Gods, eleven in number, who exist within and beyond it. These gods were the gods immanent before the creation of mortal man and mortal gods. As such they are, and remain, unmanifest; they are those 'beyond' the reckoning and sensoria of the Race of Abel; the profane flesh of clay. Az'Ra-Lumial is thus directly stated to be the 'Solely Manifest of the Eleven Elder Gods,' whose rebellion sundered Being from Non-Being.

This state is prefigured as the 'Void Place of Spirit', and the Empty Circle. It is the space wherein the solely manifest of the Elder Gods, Lumial, may ingress into the psychical and physical realm: the Circle of Witchblood. In this capacity Lumial bears forth the Spirit of the Void into conjured space, as well as sunders it so that manifestation of the Luciferian Gnosis can occur. These powers of Creation and Destruction which attend upon Lumial are clear trade marks of Lucifer throughout the ages. That they have been misunderstood and degraded as the dualistic modalities of 'good' and 'evil' reveals the blinds the Spirit of Light has cast upon the minds of the profane.

Here Lumial is called XON, the Black Light of the Void who engenders the retinues of Witchblood, the Children of Cain and the Faithful Gods of the Wise. It should be noted that XON is NOX spelled backwards—it is the Light extending from Nothing, the Night of Midnight which is the womb out of which gods are born. This Light is revealed unto man by Lumial-Xon, another example of Luciferian principle in action. Within the Draconian-Sabbatic cycle of ritual practice, this Lumial-Xon is also born within Initiated Man: eight times upon the Wheel of the Year, eight rites of the Dragon Body are celebrated within the Circles of Arte and Earth.

Each Sabbat further mantles the Supernal Serpentine Light of Lumial and gives it form.

Finally, concluding the first part of the rite, Az'Ra-Lumial descends across the Rainbow Gammadion to become the great Seven-Headed Dragon of Eld, emissary and corporeal entity of Light and Gnosis: celestial consciousness gone to earth. The Seven-Headed Dragon of Eld is the Great Dragon of Revelations represented in the heavens as the constellation of Ursa Major. The conflation of identity between the Great Bear and the Mighty Dragon has been thoroughly examined in the works of Gerald Massey, wherein he fully restores the Elder Draconian Tradition. Needless to say, the Dragon has also long been associated with Lucifer. The Dragon relates to Lumial in the Lore of the Sabbat in that both serve as intercessory spirits between heaven and earth. The seven heads are the directions of the earthly Compass; thus the Dragon-Lumial upon the earth becomes the Circle of the Royal Arte. Its mysteries are multi-dimensional in scope and arena of procession.

The second part of the Transvocation is 'Hallowing the Kingdom of the Faithful.' As mentioned previously The Lover's Call is a recension from a ritual series in *The Dragon Book of Essex* called, 'Hallowing the Kingdom of Qayin, Being the Threefold Means for Casting the Circle of the Arte Magical.' The initial practice casts a sphere of eleven directions utilizing the seed-syllables of the major Dragon Rites and their associated colors, visualized as bolts of flame. These same color attributions are used in The Lover's Call for the eight compass directions. The Zenith, Nadir and fully cast Circle are transposed to the 'Realms of Shade and Spirit', 'The Seven Lands of Earth', and 'The Star-rayed Web of Heaven', respectively. The secondary practice casts a sphere of 161 names, the names being comprised of the parts of the Dragon's Body combined with the seed syllables preceding Cain's Draconic formulary—'Azha-Ka', e.g. 'Hu Azha Ka' et al. This Elder Grammar, being the rudiments of the Serpent-Power in the Sabbatic Tradition, comprises within that realm the spheres of All-Possibility.

Finally, the third practice establishes the sphere of Eleven Gods, being the deific forms of Azhaka in the Eleven directions. Each form is visualised as possessing the limbs and ritual accoutrements of one's transformed self-image as Cain-Azhaka.

Hallowing the Kingdom of the Faithful may be seen as a fourth Circle casting in this series, as it summons the Witch-Fathers and Witch-Mothers associated with the Draconic Circle as a whole, and first manifest in the

Draconic Rite of Bha. These ward the Crooked Path entire. The Circle is bound by the Angelick Soul of Cain, Az'Ra-Lumial.

The true nature of Lumial is revealed in the Northern summons in which is written: 'Beneath my heels is the Lucifer-Stone, the Hidden centre of every land.' Here obtains the secret of the Luciferian gnosis within Cultus Sabbati. The land upon which the Seeker treads is the fallen hidden stone of Lucifer-Lumial. For the shard that fell from Lucifer's crown to earth, revitalised and re-shaped, not only its impact area but the *entirety* of the planet. In essence all the lands of the earth were made holy and sacrosanct by the Stone of Lucifer-Lumial. This is an *Arcanum Arcanorum* of the Sabbatic Cultus: that the Circle of Earth *is* become the Hidden Stone of the Light-Bringer. Hallowing the Kingdom of the Faithful is not merely a circle casting—it is a summoning of the Wards of Our Faith to open the way of the Immortal Spirit of Cain, and to bear witness to his passage through all flesh and all things.

In the sky above Lucifer-Lumial's realm are the Seven Holy Stars of the Wain, the Big Dipper, seen as the Crowned Heads of the Ancient Seven-headed Serpent of Eld. Herein is Lucifer-Lumial's celestial throne, the Pole Star, the nail that binds the twain of Earth and Heaven, and which 'never cools', meaning, it shines forever through the firmament of Time and Spirit. This nail is the veritable soul of Az'Ra-Lumial, fallen light in its initiating form, and thus is symbolic hypostate for Qayin Azhaka himself.

The 'Realms of Shade and Spirit' are governed by the composite Trinity of Man'Draku Ezh-Hou Sabatraxas. In relation to Az'Ra-Lumial they are intercessory spirits bound to the Circle of the Royal Arte: Mandraku being the spirit of the Mandrake or *Walking Man-Root*; Ezh-Hou being the ever-roaming Child who is intermediary between Men and Gods; and Sabatraxas, Toad-Daimon Initiator of Witchblood. Together as one, they ward the realms of the Mighty Witch-Dead, and as trinity comprise a hidden strand of the rite's genesis, as well as three strands of the historical reality of the Sabbbatic Current in its present phase.

The 'Seven Lands of Earth' comprise the world, whose true and only King is its wanderer, the eternal Exile and Outcast, Qayin Azhaka.

The 'Star-rayed Web of Heaven' is the completed Circle, all the realms of the Elder Gods combined and connected by the eternal soul of Az'Ra-Lumial.

The third part of the Transvocation is 'Sacrifice for Divine Assumption.' Herein Az'Ra-Lumial is called to enflesh within the sensorium of the Seeker. A 'sacrifice' is given in the form of an Oath and Pledge to pass through all things and become the Living Truth. It is sealed by the love and devotion unto Lucifer-Lumial, for in truth the entire circle-casting is an act of union with his Angelick Soul. This is why it is called 'The Lover's Call.'

The Seal is perfected in the final part in the secret Hermitage of the Seeker: his heart. His own law of freedom is declared, and the rite entire his epiphany—the *Lover's Call* to the Serpent of Light in the High Sabbat of the Ages. This is an apotheosis of the Sabbatic Cult, the transcendence of the mundane body to that of the illuminated body of starlight, known also as 'The New Flesh.'

Andrew Chumbley intended the publication of this ritual to serve as a clarion call to like-minded seekers of the Crooked Path. He understood all too well the closed nature of his Order and wanted a way to be open to those so summoned to it. In this was his generosity of spirit given and his artful cunning shown, for the rite is indeed a 'web' and many are those who have misunderstood and abused it, seeing only the masquerade of so-called Left Hand Path pathos and false idolatry. Of these, naught shall succeed, much less abide near the Throne of Lucifer. Let the true Seeker approach the rite in the knowledge of its provenance: a devotional and a hymn of praise unto the ever-living Lord of Light.

APPENDIX:
A LOVER'S CALL TO THE ANGEL OF WITCHBLOOD

I. THE FIRST CALL:
PETITION

Myself to myself I offer, this Holy Rite to begin.
By Lightning-bolt, by Flaming Torch, by the Serpent's Fire within:
Let all that I have attained in eternity by manifest in the Present Moment of I: Absolute.

O' Az-Ra-Lumial! Angelick Soul of the Master Cain!
Initiator of the Draconist Mystery, Opener of the Gates to the Crooked Path!
Hear my call, for I entreat Thee! The Vessel of the Heart is opened unto Thee!

Behold, I stand alone in Void, within the Empty Circle of the Royal Arte;
My Lover's Call goeth forth to Thee, O' Angel of the Peacock-quill!
The Lamp of the Hermit awaits the Flame of Thy Presence:
My Heart awaits the Adamantine Light of Thy initiation!

O' Az-Ra-Lumial! Solely Manifest of the Eleven Elder Gods,
Thou art XON: Light from all nullity revealed unto Man.
Thou art the Begetter of the Four Sovereign Watchers and the Sixteen Faithful Gods.

As Man thou art born—fire amidst clay—from their wiseblood and cunning seed;
Self from self, eight times Thou art begotten on the Wheel of the Year and a Day.

O' Az-Ra-Lumial, descend as Flesh, the Living Word:
The One of Light, seven times adorned in the rainbow's promise!

O' Az-Ra-Lumial, arise as Gnosis, the Mind of Heaven:
The Great Dragon, seven-headed, crowned and victorious!

II. THE SECOND CALL: HALLOWING THE KINGDOM OF THE FAITHFUL

In the North I invoke Thee in Midnight's Brightness: the Shining Darkness!
By Liliya-Devala and Mahazhael-Deval be summoned!

In the North-west I evoke Thee, in the Purple Light of Ancient Kings and Queens,
The Awakened Shades of True Ancestry! By Qinaya and Lilis be summoned!

In the West I invoke Thee, in the Indigo Light of Dusk, in the Lapis Fire of the Wards and Watchers!
By Agrath and Azhael be summoned!

In the South-west I evoke Thee, in the Azure Light of the Sky-going Gods, in the Companie of the Passionate and Free! By Qafa and Ruha be summoned!

In the South I invoke Thee, in the Emerald Light of Divine Imagination, in the Ring of Seven Mountains that edge the World-without-End! by Rahab and Azhazael be summoned!

In the South-east I evoke Thee, in the Saffron Light of the Shining Ones, by the Horns of the True and Chosen Gods! By Azh'modai and Azh'terah be summoned!

In the East I invoke Thee, in the Amber Light of the Tameless, in the Wild Procession of the Turnskin Gods! By Naamah and Zhamael be summoned!

In the North-east I evoke Thee, in the Crimson Light of all Sacrifice, in the Purified Way of Entrance that leads to the Circle of Witchblood! By Tubalo and Lucifera be summoned!

From the North I approach Thy Heart, my Lover, my Soul of Souls!
Beneath my heels is the Lucifer-Stone, the Hidden Centre of every Land.
Above me is the Circle of the Seven Holy Stars, the Crowned Heads of Thee;
In their midst is set Thy Secret Throne:
Pole of Poles, Star of Stars, the Nail that never cools!

Amid the Realms of Shade and Spirit I call to Thee,
Intercessor! Ghost-King! Sage and Jester!
Man'draku Ezh-Hou Sabatraxas! Open the Way for me!

Amid the Seven Lands of the Earth I call to Thee,
Wanderer! Loner! Witch-begetter!
Qayin Azhaka! Qayin Azhaka! Qayin Azhaka! Open the Way for me!

Amid the Star-rayed Web of Heaven I call to Thee,
Father! Mother! Initiator!
Az'Ra-Lumial! Az'Ra-Lumial! Az'Ra-Lumial! Open the Way for me!

Az'Ra-Lumial, Thy Name I recite 'til Thou art come—

III. THE THIRD CALL:
SACRIFICE FOR DIVINE ASSUMPTION

The Sphere of the Seven Rays shines all about me;
The Serpent of Seven Colours uncoils within;
The Inmost Gate is made open to Thee,
O' Az'Ra-Lumial, Spirit of Witchblood, I bid Thee enflesh!

O' Thou Spirit ruling the countless Paths of Initiation,
Open the Way for me, that I may open the Way for Thee!
This Rite is mine Oath and Pledge: in passing through all things I shall become the Living Truth.

Thus I entreat Thee O' Many-masked God of the Royal Arte,
Make Thou Thy Shrine and Hearth within me,
That I may burn with Thy Gnosis—consumed in the Perfect Love of Thee!

The Words of this Rite are as Milk, Blood and Honey to Thee.
Devotion I offer: my heart is the Rose that I lay 'pon Thine Altar.
Such are my Words, so shall it be! In Silence I go forth anew.

IV. CONTEMPLATION:
THE SEAL OF THE RITE

In Hermitage most secret, I make my decree in unsaying truth.
In Thought, Word and Deed a Wayless Fate; unique, from all paths astray;
Mine own law—ethos, aesthesis and credo—unknown to mortal gods and men.
This Rite is mine own epiphany, the Lover's Call of Apophasis: I
So Mote It Be.

Lucifer in the Lore of Old Italy

Raven Grimassi

IN ITALY THE concept of Lucifer is a multilayered one that bears both ancient and modern components. Italian writers such as Dante transformed and conflated earlier themes related to Lucifer, morphing them to fit Judeo-Christian theological themes. Dante's work was inspired by an earlier writing known as The Vision of Tundale. Peasant lore spread both old and new themes into the populace. Sorting it all out is quite an undertaking, and our best chance is to start with the roots. Doing so leads us to the realm of the stars.

From a southern European perspective the best place to begin is with the Roman idea of Lucifer. It is well established that his Latin name means 'bringer, or bearer, of light.' He was known as the morning star and as the evening star. These titles connect him with the planet Venus. In this light Lucifer is first and foremost a celestial being.

In the earlier lore about Lucifer he is associated with the sun in terms of being a herald. In this case he precedes the rising Sun. Like all beings in ancient thought, Lucifer was believed to posses a dual nature, or what the Greeks called good and evil. He was given two names: Lucifero and Noctifero. This former pointed to him in the celestial realm while the latter placed him in the Underworld. Here, Noctifero holds the dark sacred night in which light is at home in the darkness. This relates to the ancient idea that the stars, moon, and sun only visit the mortal world (passing above us) but always return to the Underworld from which they also rise.

With the establishment of Christianity, Lucifer was eventually transformed into a demon called Lucifuge (he who flees or shuns the light). This placed him permanently in the realm below, denied Lucifer his higher celestial nature, and instilled enmity between light and darkness. Here he was depicted as one of the spirits of the stars in the 'nether parts of the world' who passed influence into the roots of certain plants. These plants featured prominently in the practices of Witchcraft and Sorcery. In some latter magical systems Lucifuge was made a distinct demon, separate from Lucifer, who administrated Hell on orders of Satan.

The Judeo-Christian figure of Satan became conflated with the ancient Roman deity Lucifer due largely to the work of St. Jerome. This resulted from a series of misinterpretations of the Old Testament chapter of Isaiah, which dealt with a boastful and prideful King likened to the brightest star in the night sky (Isaiah 14:12). Here Isaiah ridicules the fallen king of Babylon in a metaphor using the Hebrew title word *helel* (meaning bright star). When the Hebrew was translated into Greek (the Septuagint Bible) the Greek name *Phosphorus* and/or *Heosphoros* (Hesperus) displaced the Hebrew term. Phosphorus meant not only 'shining bright' but also referred to the 'evening star' as a being. This changed the meaning of 'star' in the verse and moved it into that of a sentient being or entity. St. Jerome later translated the Septuagint into Latin (thereby creating the Vulgate version). In place of the Hebrew *helel*, and the Greek *Phosphorus*, St. James used the Latin word Lucifer. This tied together the themes of a bright star and a being who were one and the same. However this was not the intent of Isaiah (who knew nothing of Roman mythology or the being known as Lucifer). By connecting Lucifer with the fallen king in Isaiah, New Testament writings built upon an erroneous foundation. Biblical researcher Brian Knowles, in an essay on Lucifer, writes:

> *When he translated Isaiah 14:12, Jerome did not strictly translate the Hebrew helel ben shachar, nor did he use the Greek (LXX) Heosphoros, which term, by his day, had fallen largely into disuse. Instead he translated as though the original word had been lukophos. Lukophos, by Jerome's time, had become an epithet for the gods Apollo and Pan. Earlier, Catholic theologians Tertullian and Origen had begun to read Satan into the story of the King of Babylon in Isaiah 14. Jerome's selection of words may have been influenced by this theology.*

Another Christian theologian, St. Augustine, adds to the erroneous conflation of themes. He was responsible for creating the invalid association between Paganism/Witchcraft and the Judeo-Christian entity known as Satan. Augustine taught that Satan invented pre-Christian Pagan beliefs along with the concept of magic in order to sway people away from God. This position naturally shed a false negative light on the rival religion of Paganism, and it made it easier for the Church to work its conversion campaign. Fear of an enemy, real or imagined, has always made it easier for an organization to control people.

Here are some primary examples of the key and effective malignments used by agents of the Church:

226 CE: Origenes Adamantius (185 CE–254 CE), an important Christian scholar of the early Greek Church, and Augustine of Canterbury (d. May 26 604/605 CE), founder of the Christian Church in Southern England, both interpreted the use of the term Lucifer as a reference to the Devil.

382 CE: St. Jerome equates Lucifer with Satan in his translation of the original Hebrew and Greek writings of the Bible into Latin. In the 16th century the Council of Trent pronounced Jerome's Vulgate version of the Bible to be the authentic and authoritative Latin text of the Catholic Church. It was St. Jerome who fabricated the identification of the Roman god Lucifer with the Judeo-Christian devil figure. By shedding such a false negative light on the rival polytheistic Roman religion, an easier way was paved by the Church for its conversion campaign.

413 CE: St. Augustine equates the Judeo-Christian Satan figure with Pagan systems.

774 CE: Church equates Pagan beliefs and practices with demonic worship.

The drafting of a 'List of Superstitions' by the Council of Leptinnes in 744 fixed the identification of paganism with demonology. All survivals of pagan belief, worship, and practice were condemned as demonic and gradually suppressed by Christian theology and law. The law helped transfer the characteristics of evil spirits to human witches. The pagans had set out offerings of food and drink for minor spirits. The Synod of Rome in 743 assumed that these spirits were demons and outlawed the offerings.

The demonic spirits were then transformed into *bonae mulieres*, the ghostly 'good women' who wandered out at night going into houses and stealing food. Finally, the *bonae mulieres* were transformed into witches. Likewise, the term striga or stria, originally a blood-sucking night spirit, became a common word for a witch.[1]

TIES TO HEBREW AND MIDDLE EASTERN CONCEPTS

Italy, during the Middle Ages and Renaissance periods, experienced a flood of occult books and texts. *The Key of Solomon*, for example, appears in a 17th century Italian Witchcraft trial involving an accused woman by the name of Laura Malipiero. Her house was searched by the Capitano of the Sant' Ufficio in 1654, where a number of manuscripts were discovered. Some of these were handwritten books of spells, while others were sophisticated herbals and copies of the *Clavicle of Solomon*. In Laura's home the Inquisitors found that a copying process was taking place, and material was being distributed to interested parties. Witnesses came out against Laura, calling her the most famous witch in Venice.

Francesco Guazzo wrote in his 17th century Italian Witch Hunter's guide[2] that witches use a black book from which they read during their rites. Today many people believe that witches did not have personal books, but cases that like of Laura, and comments by such figures as Guazzo, seem to indicate otherwise.

Booksellers in Italy had been supplying prohibited books of magic and occultism for quite some time. The height of this was during a ten-year span from 1640 to 1650. The Inquisition prosecuted sellers and buyers, and the individuals on trial were as often book dealers as they were practitioners (real or imagined) of the occult arts.

The demand for occult material resulted in an influx of foreign works on hermetics, occultism, magic, and mysticism. This included material with Hebrew roots, and among the exports to Italy (and Europe in general) came material related to Biblical characters such as Cain and Abel, lore concerning Lilith, angelic beings, and Satan. One significant export that influenced modern Witchcraft is that of the Watchers.

1 Jeffrey B. Russell, *A History of Witchcraft*. Thames and Hudson Ltd., 1980.

2 *Compendium Maleficarum*, 1608.

In the ancient *Book of Enoch* we find the account of a group of angels numbering 200 who came to earth and alit upon a mountaintop. It is known by the names Mt. Armon and/or Mt. Hermon and is located on the border of what is now Syria and Lebanon. The angels, known as the Watchers, were led by an angel called Samyaza in one account and by Azazel in another. In 300 BCE a temple to the god Pan stood on the slopes of Mt. Hermon. This may point to a connection between the god Pan and the angel Azazel (who was himself associated with a goat in ancient Hebrew practices).

Azazel appears only once in the Bible in a passage describing a ritual (Leviticus, chapter 16). Here we find the offering in the form of a goat, who as a scapegoat for the sins of the people, is killed to make atonement with God. In some of the lore associated with this rite is the depiction of the goat being tossed from a mountain cliff. Some commentators see in this a link to the mountain on which the Watchers are said to have arrived on earth.

It is difficult to sort out Hebraic influences from foundational European elements of Western witchcraft. Before the arrival of foreign writings and teachings, European paganism had no personification of evil in the form of a goddess or god. Instead, all deities possessed a dual nature, and just like the forces of Nature the actions of the gods could be either beneficial or destructive.

When we look at Southern European witchcraft, we find the image of a black goat who wears a candle or a torch between the horns on his head. Within the sect this candle represented the light of Lucifer, the shining star in the night. This imagery is reflected in the now famous figure of the Sabbatic goat popularized by Eliphas Levi's drawing in his book *Transcendental Magic.*

Witch Hunter Guazzo, in his *Compendium Maleficarum*, mentions that in 1594 a young girl confessed to having been "corrupted at a tender age by a certain Italian" who took her out into a field one night. Here the man traced a circle on the ground with a beech twig. Immediately following this act, the girl was approached by two women who had with them a black goat with large horns. Next to arrive was a man dressed like a priest. The young girl claimed that the goat asked the Italian who she was, and that he replied she had been brought to join the fellowship.

A simple rite of veneration followed in which a black candle was fixed between the goat's horns. Everyone came forward and lit their candles from its flame. This was followed by acts of worship (no detailed description) and ended with the attendants dropping coins into a bowl. The second time the young girl was taken to the field; she claimed that the goat asked for a lock of her hair, which the Italian then snipped from her head. The lock of hair was then given to the goat. Next, according to the girl, a ritual followed in which she became the goat's bride. According to her, she was led into the woods where the goat pressed her to the ground and then sexually penetrated her.

This is one of the less 'supernatural' accounts of the witches' gatherings, and it has some realistic elements in terms of old lore related to witchcraft. Noteworthy is the inclusion of a black candle, which reflects what is called the Devil's candle or an Elf lantern, which is a black candle wrapped in mandrake leaves. Its placement between the horns of the goat is connected to old rites in which a candle was placed on a Y-shaped staff or stang. The evening-star was first 'sighted' through the branches, and then the star was fixed to it by the lighted candle. In this theme, Lucifer descends from the heavens to the earth. Later this is seen as the fallen angel in Christian ideas, and here the Devil is introduced into Witchcraft.

In some forms of peasant magic in Italy, the Devil is incorporated to empower spells. One example shows up in the practices of a Sicilian woman named Vanna, who is written about in a book titled *By-Paths in Sicily* by Eliza Putnam Heaton.[3] Vanna is asked why she calls upon the Devil, and her reply is because he has much power.

Vanna evokes the Devil, referring to him as a Saint:

Saint Devil, concede me what I wish.
I will not respect you Devil,
If you do not concede me what I wish.
I will respect you as Devil,
When you concede me what I wish

In the formal evocation of the Devil, Vanna looks for a certain star, and then continues her incantation, which in this case is for a love spell to compel a man named Peppino:

Shining star, powerful star,
Heedless of me still you are?
Bright angel of the good light,

3 E. P. Dutton & Company, New York, 1920.

In three words bring him to my sight.
Well come, well go; take him by the feet.
Devil of Mt. Etna dread,
Peppino seize by the hairs of his head,
Thou Devil of the mouth awry,
Peppino take and bring him nigh...

The Devil features prominently during the era of witchcraft trials as a male figure of veneration; curiously we can find no pre-Christian connection to a clear 'god of witchcraft' in early writings. It is as though he remained invisible, but there may be some sense to this as we look deeper back into the past.

Several years ago I set out to try and discover pre-Christian references to a god of witchcraft. References to various goddesses were plentiful enough, but I found nothing directly revealing a god. Among the earliest goddesses mentioned, the most frequent and prominent are Hecate, Diana, and Proserpina. None of these were connected to any consort in literary sources, and therefore, no trail presented itself that I could follow in search of a god of witchcraft linked to any of these goddesses. It was as though he was invisible.

Hecate is the oldest goddess name associated with witches and witchcraft in Western literature. This fact seemed like a logical place to start the hunt. One of the things that stand out in archaic elements of her veneration is the crossroads. In ancient times a tree trunk called a *hekataion*, which stood in the center of three crossing paths, denoted her presence at the crossroads. In time the tradition of setting a trunk turned to that of erecting a stone pillar.

Stone pillars set at crossroads became attached to a term known as a *herms*. In its earliest form it was just a crudely carved column with a square base. Later on, the herms was carved to include a humanoid bust atop the column. The early tradition called for travelers on the roads to leave some collected rocks near the herms. These were in turn used by the road builders to repair and extend the roads. Merchants and suppliers used these roads for commerce.

Surviving images carved on the herms reveal to us that the busts are the gods known as Priapus and Hermes. Of the two, Hermes is connected to Hecate. Both deities are associated with the crossroads, souls of the dead, and passage between the world of the living and the dead. Scholar Karl

Kerenyi describes Hecate and Hermes as 'secret lovers,'[4] and they share an intimate connection to Otherworld themes. The idea of Hermes in such a close relationship with the classic goddess of witchcraft is very noteworthy.

In his earliest form, Hermes is a god of cattle. These were important animals used in commerce, and so Hermes became connected to commercial ventures. By extension, he was also associated with the roads used for commerce. As a god of cattle, is it possible that the winged helmet we often see him wearing is an image evolved from an earlier crown with two horns? In the earliest depictions of Greek art it is not clear what the protrusions are on his headwear. However, in later periods they are certainly wings.

In the myths and legends associated with Hermes we find a magical helmet that makes him invisible. I was intrigued by the idea of an invisible god in light of the fact I could not 'see' a god of witchcraft in pre-Christian literature. This motivated me to look further into the nature and character of Hermes.

As I continued my investigation, Hermes began to emerge as an incredibly archaic deity. He is associated with time and with the stars. In Kerenyi's book *Hermes, Guide of Souls* we find an ancient depiction of Hermes wearing a black cloak covered with stars.[5] He sports a beard and carries a short crook. This is in sharp contrast to the later images in which we find him youthful and clean-shaven.

In the Christian era Hermes became identified with Satan; perhaps this was due to his nature as a trickster in ancient myth. Some scholars suggest that the winged devil image of the Middle Ages was inspired by the wings borne by Hermes in Greek art. The Devil's pitchfork may also be derived from the caduceus held by Hermes, which resembles a trident. Hermes is associated with escorting souls of the dead to the Underworld, and the Devil is depicting as ensnaring them and holding them in hell.

Among the interesting connections to Hermes is the invention of musical instruments. In one tale he invents the lyre for Apollo and the flute for Pan. This is noteworthy in light of a continuing superstition among musicians. An old custom is to go to the crossroads and make a deal with the Devil in exchange for increased musical talent. As noted earlier, Hermes is intimately connected to the crossroads. Is this a coincidence?

Near the end of my search for pre-Christian references to a god of witchcraft, I remembered a curious image. It is not from this early period,

4 Karl Kerenyi, *Hermes, Guide of Souls.* (Spring Publications, 2008) pp 84–85.

5 Karl Kerenyi, *Hermes, Guide of Souls.* (Spring Publications, 2008) frontispiece.

but it bears a symbol that cannot be ignored. The image is that of the Sabbatic Goat, also known as Baphomet. Upon examining the figure, a phallus is clearly present and is in the form of the caduceus of Hermes. Could the Sabbatic Goat be a form of Hermes associated with witchcraft? When we factor in that one of Hermes' cult animals is a goat, the question becomes more intriguing.

One of the early accusations against witches in the Christian era is that they gathered to commune with spirits of the dead at the crossroads. Hermes is also a god of communication and messages. In ancient times Hecate and Hermes were the primary deities connected to the setting of the crossroads and the theme of spirit contact. Hecate is the Gatekeeper to the Underworld, and Hermes is the escort of the dead. What better deity to call upon when working with invisible spirits of the dead than an invisible god?

LUCIFER IN ITALIAN WITCHCRAFT

The figure of Lucifer in Italian witchcraft is perhaps best known to the public through the writings of folklorist Charles Godfrey Leland. In Leland's book *Aradia*, Lucifer is identified with the Judeo-Christian myth of Satan being expelled from heaven due to the 'sin' of pride. In Italian mainstream culture the ideas about Lucifer were strongly influenced by the fictional tale of Dante, which describes Lucifer in vivid detail. But these are all ideas about Lucifer from the perspective of the Church and its agents.

In order to obtain a non-Christianized view of Lucifer we need to examine tales of Lucifer that have no attachment to stereotypical imagery. One example is the witch lore that was passed to me many years ago. In one story Lucifer is known as Lucifero, and is seen as the brightest star in the night sky. The 'star' is known today as the planet Venus. In the old tale, Lucifer moves to join with the crescent moon, which is the goddess Diana Lucifera. This is represented by Venus positioned near the crescent moon at night. Diana is impregnated by Lucifer, and she later births stars to replace those that have fallen to earth. The stars are the offspring of Lucifer and Diana Lucifera.

The idea of a 'fallen' Lucifer may originate from an old tale in which Lucifer descends from the heavens (as opposed to being cast out) and lands with such force that he penetrates into the earth. His presence in the Underworld produces volcanic activity, and for this reason pumice stones are sometimes called Devil's Rock in some forms of Catholic-based folk magic.

In the witch lore passed to me, the symbol of a five-pointed star enclosed in a circle, with one point downward, symbolizes Lucifer within the earth. With one point upward, the enclosed star symbolizes the union of Lucifer and Diana Lucifera. It also represents the 'star child' who is the 'seed of enlightenment and liberation' within Diana's womb or within the womb of the earth. From this come such ideas as Lucifer and Diana being the parents of the Witch Queen, Aradia.

In the peasant witchcraft tradition, Lucifer is tied to the firefly or lightning bug, which in Italy is known as the *lucciola*. In the old mythos these are the 'stars' of the harvest field touching the wheat spikes that are ready for harvesting. However, in this theme Lucifer is known as Lucibello, the beautiful light. The lucciola are the stars that have descended from the sky (the falling stars) who are under the guidance of Lucibello. This, of course, connects back to the impregnation of Diana Lucifera by Lucifero in the night sky. A type of 'as above, so below' theme.

In some Italian witchcraft traditions Diana is known as the Queen of the Fairies. In this mythos the lucciola appear in folklore as fairies who gather on the night of the summer solstice. In the mystical tradition, wheat spikes hold the mysteries of the Underworld, which were drawn up by the roots of the plants. The lucciola, as a fairy spirit, lands on the tips of the wheat spike and imparts the mysteries of the star realm. The descended star-beings below the earth pass their secret knowledge into the roots of the wheat. Later the wheat will be used to make ritual bread that is used in a type of communion meal through which the inner mysteries are taken into the body, mind and spirit of the ritualists. The words of communion illustrate the mystical process:

> *Blessings upon this meal, which is as our own body. For without this, we ourselves would perish from this world. Blessings upon the grain, which as seed went into the earth where deep secrets hide. And there did dance with the elements, and spring forth as flowered plant, concealing secrets strange. When you were in the ear of grain, spirits of the field came to cast their light upon you, and aid you in your growth. Thus through you we shall be touched by that same Race, and the mysteries hidden within you, we shall obtain even unto the last of these grains.*

The Gain Mysteries are associated with Lucifero (who beneath the earth is known as Noctifer or Nottambulo (the Night Walker). The light of the stars in the Underworld, emanating from Lucifer, give illumination in every sense of the word. It is the mystery teaching that light is at home in the darkness–literally, enlightenment in the places of darkness. Night-walking leads to the discovery of light in the hidden realm.

Lucifero is the *star seeder*, the light of renewal, just as Lucibello is the *renewer* of light at the mating of fireflies in the wheat fields on the summer solstice. He offers light and enlightenment wherever it is absent, and he is the revealer of the hidden mysteries. It is through his descent to earth, and his penetration into the dark realm below, that Lucifero impregnates the earth with revealing light. The falling stars that connect with his mythos are sometimes regarded as his allies or fellow star beings that join him on the earth.

Fragmented elements of what can be called the *Lucifero Mysteries* peer out from several popular pieces of Italian literature. One interesting account is found in the writings of a man named Matteo Palmieri. On August eve, in 1451, he dreamed that his dead friend Cipriano Rucellai appeared to him with an invitation to join him on a trip to the yearly festival celebrated on the first of August. The festival was known as Il Paradiso and was held near Florence. In his dream, Matteo accompanied the ghost of Cipriano to the festival, and along the way they speak about the state of spirits after death. The conversation includes where they dwell, and how they are permitted to revisit the living.

During the discussion, Cipriano revealed various matters to Palmieri concerning the nature of the human soul. He told him how God first created hosts of angels separated into three companies. One group followed Lucifer, when he rebelled. The second group held fast to the angel Michael and affirmed their allegiance. The third group did not side with God or with Lucifer. After Lucifer's departure, the angels of the third group were then relegated to the Elysian Fields. In the matter of the third class of angels, God desired to give them a final chance to choose sides, which he designated as good and evil. God ordained that each angel in the group is to be sent, one by one, to dwell in human bodies. The angels are allowed to choose their lives on the earth, and are accompanied by a good and a bad spirit. After the death of the inhabited body, each angel is then drafted into the company of Lucifer or Michael according to their conduct during the material life. Palmieri composed a poem titled *tersa rima,* which details the conversation in his dream.

Palmieri's dream ties in with the teachings regarding a class of beings in Italian witchcraft known as the *Grigori*. The name is rooted in the Italian word *grigio*, which means gray, and in this light the Grigori are the Grey Ones (neither black or white). In the Italic mythos of these Grigori, they first appear to humans from a gray mist. As previously noted, in Hebrew angelic lore there is a class of angels called the Grigori who are also known as the Watchers. These beings feature prominently in several modern systems of witchcraft and Wicca.

Lucifero is not directly connected to the Grigori in Italian witchcraft, but he does share the stellar associations. In other words he is not named as their leader, and he is not identified as one of the Grigori. As a figure in Italian witchcraft, Lucifer has evolved over the centuries, during which time Christian elements were added to the non-Christian origins of his mythos. By the time of the writings of Charles Leland, Lucifer appears to be identified (in some circles) with the Judeo-Christian devil mythos. It may be that certain groups of witches venerated this depiction of Lucifer, but others did not.

As Christian influences found their way into Italian witchcraft, such elements as Saint veneration helped create a detour from the non-Christian Lucifer over to the Christian one. Some groups embraced the Christian elements and integrated them into a new form of the Old Craft, which came to be called Stregoneria. The Old Ways maintained the non-Christian understanding and continued on as Stregheria (the Old Religion). However, by Leland's era the waters were well muddied, and this resulted in much of the confusion we have today about Italian witchcraft traditions. Likewise it leaves things ripe for a misunderstanding of Lucifer as an entity as well as a figure featured in witchcraft.

The Lucifer Moment

Lee Morgan

To conceal while it reveals is always the characteristic of the myth. The drama transports us to the very confines of the world of sense, where material semblance trembles into spiritual truth; but the limit is never quite crossed, the reticence of the image is never forfeited...The imagination everywhere suggests what the intellect cannot define.

—Vida D. Scudder

INTRODUCTION

In his 1892 preface to *Prometheus Unbound,*[1] Scudder speaks of a 'mythic quality' that emerges in certain periods of history, times when new myths are suddenly able to bubble to the surface of collective awareness. Or instead when old myths could be dissolved, calcified, coagulated and recombined in new convolutions.

He speaks of how 'myth is almost entirely confined to the childhood of races', which to the modern ear sounds redolent of cultural Darwinism. But then Scudder observes that this youthful vigour returns at such mythic periods in history, in a cyclic reemergence.[2]

1 (ed) Vida D. Scudder, *Prometheus Unbound: A Lyrical Drama*, by P. B. Shelley, D. C. Heath and co. 1906, p. 27

2 This is reminiscent of Rudolf Steiner's Anthroposophical concept about the Luciferic principle as the expansive, vigorous power that pushes against the Ahrimanic forces of constriction, tradition, and inertia. Using Steiner's terminology you might say that Scudder is expressing the belief that these cyclic returns of the mythic quality are Luciferic upsurges.

> *Through our own oldest epic, Beowulf, even yet flash traces of the myth; but they soon fade out...replaced by the frank and sunny naturalism of Chaucer, Shakespeare, and Browning. [Yet] In the early days of our own century, when the English race had passed through many a stern experience, when it had gathered much of the bitter wisdom of maturity into its thought and speech, once more it was to dream dreams and see visions, and the fairest of these dreams was to be given to the world through the poet-soul of Shelley, a genuine and beautiful myth, in the form of the Prometheus Unbound.*[3]

What was this new myth of Shelley's, at its essence, if not a deeply Luciferic retelling of the Prometheus myth, with Zeus as a flimsy cover for the Demiurge? This Promethean figure, Milton's Lucifer, and the figure of the Wandering Jew all haunt the imaginal landscape of the nineteenth century, whispering to a world on the edge of industrial modernity, telling of the outsider's perspective.

The devil, one might say, to alter Shelley's famous quote, owes everything to literature. He had a very small part in the Bible and yet into this decidedly unbiblical figure so much mythic power has migrated and settled. His dramas have not been played out inside churches and scriptures but inside playhouses, fireside tales and in old poems. So it only makes sense to go looking for Lucifer among the pages of dusty books, haunted libraries, and the twisted corridors of the imagination where man has always had more liberty to ask dangerous questions than he has outside it.

LUCIFER UNBOUND

I want to tell a story about poets that reshaped myths that still affects our current episteme, the occult world, and the way we understand the figure of Lucifer today. But first we will burrow deeper into the depth-meaning of the word, episteme. What is an episteme? And how do you know when you've broken one?

When the philosopher Michel Foucault tried to explain how the mindset of people from other epistemes can be *literally unthinkable* he used the example of a tale from the Argentinean writer Borges about a supposed Chinese encyclopedia that classifies animals as:

3 Scudder, op cit, p. 13

> *(a) belonging to the Emperor, (b) embalmed, (c) tame, (d) sucking pigs, (e) sirens, (f) fabulous, (g) stray dogs, (h) included in the present classification, (i) frenzied, (j) innumerable, (k) drawn with a very fine camel hair brush, (l) et cetera, (m) having just broken the water pitcher, (n) that from a long way off look like flies.*[4]

There are so many things about this taxonomy that strike us as foreign that the immediate response is humour. Humour can be a wonderful way of letting off tension when we uncover the unthinkable, the unexpected and the unframable.

Like Lucifer, the Chinese encyclopedia disturbs our sense of order itself, a sense we aren't even aware of having until we feel it violated by absurdity. When you are hunting for the traces and echoes that a mystery leaves behind, the absent or the silent thing, the unnoticed, the rejected, is often more salient than all of the most evident facts. What things in life disturb us in this manner? Allow us to see things that have been invisible through familiarity and invite us to consider what things looks like from outside our paradigm?

If you have felt something that violates your sense of knowledge about the universe and disturbs all that is familiar to you, then you has met Lucifer. Through his rebellion, and his resistance, he allows us to perceive the quality of the invisible episteme around us in ways that everyone else living and churning in the guts of the system do not. This insight alone can grant power, to be awake inside our own systemic reality is to be able to manipulate it. Without a disruption, an emergence of the Other, or outrage to the existing paradigm, the episteme in which we live remains invisible and we its automatons.

Lucifer exists within every intellectual outrage, the ultimate *aporia,*[5] the moment of total cognitive dissonance that anyone experiences when something pierces their worldview with information they can't assimilate into previous frameworks. Even for those who would never admit to His existence as a spiritual entity, most thinking people have felt Him nonetheless.

4 Michel Foucault, *The Order of Things: An Archeology of the Human Sciences,* Pantheon Books, 1970, p. 1.

5 In philosophy, an aporia is a philosophical puzzle or a seemingly insoluble impasse in an inquiry. It can also denote the state of being perplexed, or at a loss, at such a puzzle or impasse.

Some ages have laughed at Him in their certainty of their culture's absolutes, just as we laugh at the strangeness of the Chinese taxonomy. Laughter is merely one way of dealing with the discomfort of Lucifer, the sand who through irritation creates the pearl in the belly of oysters. Other eras and individuals felt great fear of him and did not laugh, others a kind of frightened desire that touched the edges of the poetic sublime. The poets of the early nineteenth century, this time of mythic reemergence, show evidence of all three responses; this is how we know they are great poets. Because a poet can best be assessed by how many 'Lucifer moments' they manage and facilitate for others.

Today in our fast-food, fast entertainment world the sense of an alliance between poets and the devil has been all but lost along with the air of anti-social danger the art once carried. And yet, unheedingly we consume the watered down fruit of their long spent inspiration, in every anti-hero and romantic Luciferic figure that graces page and screen.

It didn't pay to be the ultimate manifestation of evil in a world of black and white, or worse still, to be the ultimate manifestation of ambiguity in an absolute world. For to the absolutist, uncertainty and liminality itself is the essence of evil. But when the world changed Lucifer was always ready, as he always is, lurking in the threshold spaces between sign and signified, ready to stretch our boundaries and explode our frames of reference.

When you read a text that takes you entirely outside of your paradigms for a dizzying second you see with the eyes of the Other and look back on all that is familiar to you and deem it alien and new, we might call this the 'Lucifer moment'. Bringing forth these moments in the reader is the sacred task of all literature, that which cannot give us a fresh pair of eyes for a moment is mere entertainment.

It was part of the way through the eighteenth century when Lucifer decided he'd like to smash through the old epoch and change his skin again. He didn't seem to care when they laughed at him in earlier times, and made him the bumbler of their tales, or the subject of their hunts, he was always a man with an eye for the main chance. Fast to don a new mask and enter the stage with the flamboyance of Goethe's Mephistopheles, or the dramatic intensity of Milton's Satan. It was in the form of Milton's Lucifer, after being imaginatively dormant for a few hundred years, that he found his way, like a stranger at the door, to the consciousnesses of the young Romantic poets.

When Milton wrote *Paradise Lost* he claimed that he meant to defend God's actions to man, in accordance with Christian dogma. But that was before revolution had torn a hole through everything that seemed certain, where history itself was busy providing the world with Lucifer moments.

In a world where kings, queens and nobility could be taken down to the guillotine, where kings could be *wrong*, could not the demiurge also be wrong? Was it not time to introduce a little ambiguity to his legendary opponent? How could the poet of this era not respond to the scent of Luciferic chaos in the air?

In W. H. Abrams famous *The Mirror and the Lamp*[6] he provided evidence of a transformation that begun in the mind of the Romantics where creativity went from being mirror-like, in that the writer could only reflect back their society and environment, to becoming more like a lamp. The inspired writer or poet was now a light source, a creative wellspring from within, a personage who embodied revolution, -that is, the poet had themselves become a Lucifer moment.

This meant a quiet *coup de grace* was occurring. Once this change in the episteme was fully established the function of literature was no longer strictly to uphold the dominant paradigm but to inject chaotic newness. Poetry and literature, the creative act itself, in fact, was becoming explicitly Luciferic. From this point on in history Lucifer no longer belonged only to the people and the playhouse, he had made a run on high culture and established himself in a fine greatcoat and open-necked shirt.

The immediate thing that Lucifer is associated with is light, but in literature he is obviously associated with darkness also. Sadly, very few of us will really be able to appreciate what darkness and light actually meant to our forebears. Such fundamentals are so familiar to us as to have become invisible; when we talk about them we tend to act as mirrors when to really understand their significance we must think not as 'mirrors' but as 'lamps.'

The closest thing we can do to cut through all epistemic difference is to return to the primal experience of light and dark for our species, to imaginatively feel into the campfire and the wild-animal tooth-bearing darkness beyond the tree line. We must imagine into the fragility of the light when all we have is the tiny stub of tallow candle left to last the evening and wolves howl in the woods outside. In winter the darkness would seem to go on and on...As a belief-figure of the Western imaginal Lucifer has always straddled these potent realms that tug at the root and core of what it means to be human. He rides the wild ululations of the wolf from the

6 W. H. Abrams, *The Mirror and the Lamp: Romantic Theory and the Critical Tradition*, Oxford University Press, 1971.

trees outside threatening your way of life, but he also brings the unstable fire of civilization that burns in the hearth and the mind and sparks riots and revelations. He reveals the double-edged sword of fire, to those cunning enough to understand, and he reveals the fertile darkness in which it must always be plunged. Yet if we will not heed or respect that darkness that makes us uncomfortable, he's just as willing to let us burn our fingers on his flame.

So far though, we have spoken of Lucifer as if he were ever one individual, when we should speak of 'Lucifers.' From the moment the figure of Lucifer became attached in early witchcraft narrative to the being that lives behind the folk devil of witches we find many Lucifers, some that express more of his rustic heritage, others that show his 'gentleman in the black suit' visage.

These many devils are reflexes of Lucifer's (or are they perhaps a reflex of our response to his power, as revealed in the aporia moment where sense becomes nonsense?) that seem to pull new scapegoats into the mesh of its power story. By the late eighteenth to early nineteen century the poet was beginning to take on many of these scapegoat characteristics of the sacred yet profane outsider, the Wandering Jew and the outcast bearing the Mark of Cain. They were coming to be a lamp rather than a mirror, they were becoming Lucifers. Or was Lucifer becoming them?

Like all tropes that have been there before we were born we tend to think of the notion that poets, artists and creative genius' of all stamps are likely to be disturbed, tortured souls who die young as being an eternal one, when in reality this concept only has a couple of hundred years of history and this is how it began—somewhere in what the Romantic imagination did with the concept of Milton's tragic anti-hero, Lucifer.

In academic circles literary critics laugh at this concept of the tortured genius now, seeing it as the very hallmark of Romantic age naivety. Meanwhile the migration of our culture's needs for expiation and sacrifice onto lesser social figures continues largely unexamined and unabated in the cult of celebrity. We may not tear celebrities limb from limb but the pursuit of Princess Diana by the paparazzi is the closest thing to a Bacchanalia sacrifice we are likely to see in this era. Popular culture has swallowed up mankind's need to venerate and destroy an idol in Dionysian frenzy and absorbed it into the cult of stardom—a state which itself was first embodied by a poet.[7]

7 Lord Byron is usually reckoned the 'first celebrity' in the modern sense, complete

So rather than speaking of dry historical dates let us slide into this teeming, humid imaginal space created by the poets, into the places and faces created by them to house all the homeless gods, spectres, monsters, faeries, sirens, hobgoblins, headless horsemen, washers at the ford, witch hares and boggarts that had been taken from them by the rise of rationalism. We must go beyond the familiarity of their voices that have been made to seem dry by endless repetition in English classes. Another powerful tool the modern world has devised to combat the Lucifer moment is this ability to study something until the hot blood of its vitality harrows up into a dry powder. Once these words were electric to the ear.

This is what happened to the devil between Milton and Hugo. He was standing before us the whole time beggar, bawd, poet, thief, thinker, revolutionary, tinker, hero, scorned one... Seeming to say to us 'rejoice and despair at once for everything must happen!' Literature became a release valve that knew how to let just enough of his rapturous complexity spill out, and how to keep just enough tucked safely away to boil and bubble up the essence of future Zeitgeists.

So rather than seeing the following works as evidence of societies rigid projections about Lucifer, I'd rather we opened our mind's eye to seeing these texts as a conduit via which The Light Bringer has been able to erupt into the minds of man. Let us not be trapped imagining that literature was ever anything less than a high stakes game at who would control the myths of the era... The hand that writes the texts that cradle us, rocks the world...

Lucifer is ever the Other, The Stranger, the Abject. Thus he will come clothed in the way that shocks yet beguiles the Zeitgeist, that rouses and confronts the reader. Lucifer speaks with a thousand tongues, quills, pens and keyboards. He'll nail his bold vision to the door and then laugh at you while you take it too seriously. Goethe's Mephistopheles knew something of this, but it was Milton, as appreciated hundreds of years after his death in a way he claims he did not intend, who helped make a dramatic, tragic, courageous and dignified (if not yet sympathetic) devil 'thinkable'.

By the early 19th century the English Romantic P. B. Shelley declared:

> *Nothing can exceed the energy and magnificence of the character of Satan. It is a mistake to suppose that he could ever have been intended for the popular personification of evil.*[8]

with Byron watchers with binoculars hiding in bushes.

8 P.B Shelley, *A Defence of Poetry*, Watts and co., 1915, p.103.

He even went so far as to add in the same paragraph that Milton's Satan, as a moral being, was superior to God. This is hardly surprising given many of the philosophical resonances that Lucifer of Paradise Lost shares with Shelley's epoch. When Milton's Lucifer, cast down into Hell for his disobedience to God, says:

> *Hail, horrors! Hail Infernal world! And thou, profoundest Hell, receive thy new possessor—one who brings a mind not to be changed by place or time. The mind is its own place, and in itself can make a Heaven of Hell, a Hell of Heaven.*

He speaks almost the key philosophical mood of the future, a mindset that speaks not only of revolutions in the political sphere, but revolutions of the mind, intellectual worlds turned upside down.

By the time Goethe wrote *Faust* the perspective on Lucifer was notably different from Milton in its stated intent. Goethe claimed that he had purposely written a passage in Faust 'where the devil himself received grace from god.[9] This notion, that Lucifer himself may receive grace, may even Himself be saved, cuts close to making the devil seem a necessary part of all goodness and if one follows the implications of that line of thought to its conclusion, the ultimate sacrificial scapegoat.

Goethe's Mephistopheles is not 'the devil' but a devil, and is nonetheless attached to a web of archetypical associations that chart the devil's imaginative life throughout history. Sometimes he is absurd, sometimes he is terrible, yet the origin story this devil gives in *Faust* places his existence as primeval and first before the coming of the light.

> *Part of the part am I, which at the first was all,*
> *A part of darkness, which gave birth to light,*
> *Proud light, who now his mother would enthrall,*
> *Contesting space and ancient rank with night.*
> *Yet he succeedeth not, for struggle as he will,*
> *To forms material he adhereth still;*
> *From them he streameth, them he maketh fair,*
> *And still the progress of his beams they check;*
> *And so, I trust, when comes the final wreck,*
> *Light will, ere long, the doom of matter share.*

9 Maximilian Rudwin, '*The Salvation of Satan in Modern Poetry*', *The Open Court Magazine*, Vol. XLV, 1931, p. 73.

Interestingly the primordial darkness 'gives birth' to light, suggesting not only the supremely heretical idea that the devil's existence precedes that of God, but the darkness that Mephistopheles equates with himself has a feminine gender. Light, who ostensibly is connected with the Demiurge is clearly a 'he' who is the one charged with pride against his mother darkness. Right from this point an astute reader can perceive the distance we have come since Milton wrote his drama to defend the rule of God. We can see that the poet of this new era was beginning to feel a right to suggest anarchic new mythological interpretations of major religious figures. This points towards a strong secularization of religious thought and experience.

We see also the imaginative mark of early modernity that comes to suspect the light's ambiguity. Mary Shelley's Frankenstein and the Prometheus figures of the Romantics have much in common in this respect. Images of both light and darkness as positive or potentially negative forces abound in the writing of this era. Darkness can be terrible and world ending as in Byron's poem *Darkness*, but there are also love poems to death and darkness. It is light in the form of electricity, a refinement of the Promethean fire that brings Mary Shelley's monster of modern hubris to birth, and in her work we find perhaps the ultimate critique of false or unbalanced light.

It could easily be said that the stirrings of the modern mind when we stopped fearing the darkness so exclusively and began to worry about our ever increasing harnessing of light. What happens when there is too much light, what if we need darkness? What if the dark things inside ourselves are starving? In the first flickerings of this fear of the false light of uncheck progress we have the seeds of all modern counter cultural movements.

Milton had certainly made his Satan speak of hell as a state of mind and the power of the mind, but in *Faust* Goethe virtually expresses the ideal of Left Hand Path occultism, as well as the scapegoat element of the becoming a Lucifer:

Whatever is the lot of humankind
I want to taste within my deepest self.
I want to seize the highest and the lowest,
to load its woe and bliss upon my breast,
and thus expand my single self titanically
and in the end go down with all the rest.

If we are to fully comprehend Goethe's devil figure, then we must know his Demiurge. For all of the Romantics and proto-Romantics the Demiurge is a mixture of Jehovah and Zeus/Jupiter. By the time of the French Revolution he was usually characterized as heartless. This can all be explained away as words placed in the mouth of Satan that the writer does not expect us to agree with, or can it? What is harder to explain away is the increasing mentions of a force more ancient than the Demiurge.

For Goethe it was *Das Mutters* (The Mothers), for Shelley it was Demigorgon, these titanic Fate figures seem to be part of the darkness that proceeded the light, as in Mephistopheles' origin story. To Goethe *Das Mutters* represented a force so primordial it couldn't be properly spoken of—which always suggests one is touching on a reality outside one's own episteme. Famously, when asked: who are Das Mutters?, Goethe would only throw his hands up in frustration and cry: "*Das Mutters!*"

Something dark and implacable was finding its way into the work of this period, something that gave away a new deeper truth, that the Lucifer moment didn't only come on like a light in the darkness, it crept up like a dark memory of the hidden life of inscrutable Nature.

Just when it seemed that Milton's aristocratic devil had set the lens through which the new Lucifer would be understood, we find the rustic folkloric devil in all his glory, but with new Romantic sympathy, portrayed by the poet Robbie Burns. Worth quoting at length for its folklore content:

'O thou! whatever title suit thee,—Auld Hornie, Satan, Nick, or Clootie! Wha in yon cavern, grim an' sootie,' Burns begins, addressing Lucifer with names traditional to his area and more general.

I've heard my rev'rend graunie say,
In lanely glens ye like to stray;
Or whare auld ruin'd castles gray
Nod to the moon,
Ye fright the nightly wand'rer's way
Wi' eldritch croon.

When twilight did my graunie summon
To say her pray'rs, douce honest woman!
Aft yont the dike she's heard you bummin,
Wi' eerie drone;
Or, rustlin thro' the boortrees comin,
Wi' heavy groan.

Ae dreary, windy, winter night,
The stars shot down wi' sklentin light,
Wi' you mysel I gat a fright,
Ayont the lough;
Ye like a rash-buss stood in sight,
Wi' waving sugh.

The cudgel in my nieve did shake,
Each bristl'd hair stood like a stake,
When wi' an eldritch, stoor "Quaick, quaick,"
Amang the springs,
Awa ye squatter'd like a drake,
On whistling wings.

Let warlocks grim an' wither'd hags
Tell how wi' you on ragweed nags
They skim the muirs an' dizzy crags
Wi' wicked speed;
And in kirk-yards renew their leagues,
Owre howket dead...

When thowes dissolve the snawy hoord,
An' float the jinglin icy-boord,
Then water-kelpies haunt the foord
By your direction,
An' nighted trav'lers are allur'd
To their destruction.

And aft your moss-traversing spunkies
Decoy the wight that late an drunk is:
The bleezin, curst, mischievous monkeys
Delude his eyes,
Till in some miry slough he sunk is,
Ne'er mair to rise.

When Masons' mystic word an grip
In storms an' tempests raise you up,
Some cock or cat your rage maun stop,
Or, strange to tell!

The youngest brither ye wad whip
Aff straught to hell!

But fare you weel, Auld Nickie-ben!
O wad ye tak a thought an' men'!
Ye aiblins might—I dinna ken—
Still hae a stake:
I'm wae to think upo' yon den,
Ev'n for your sake!

Here Burns seems to describe a personal vision of the devil, describing him as like sighing reeds in the wind, causing his hairs to stand on end. The devil then departs on whistling wings, making a 'squattering' sound like a drake. There is something immensely strange about this description that is far more than rehearsed tradition and seems flecked through with authenticity.

Here 'Auld Hornie' is presented as the head of all punkies and water sprites, giving him clear dominion over the non-Christian spirit world of Scotland. But it is at the end when Burns expresses sympathy 'even for his sake', and asks him to spare a thought for men, that we see the radicalism of his era echoing most plainly.

A kind of unconscious heretical Gnosticism seeps through the writing of this period, and the Demiurge becomes the tyrannical power of the episteme, not just representing earthly kings, but of the dominant model of reality. Romanticism was never just about a war of classes, but a war in the mind, a war for the dominant myth of the era. Before the Romantics the Demiurge was manifest in the King, after the Romantic age the Demiurge forever after would be cognate with the ideas that rule us. Romanticism as a syntactic producer of reality had begun to become conscious of being conscious.

Lucifer can only be understood through knowing the nature of the Demiurge, and visa versa. In this sense Goethe's Luciferic projections are linked to those of the younger Romantics via the figure of Prometheus. Because it was less confronting to the mainstream to cast criticism at 'Zeus' rather than Jehovah, the Demiurge of the nineteenth century is well depicted by the poets as the enemy of Prometheus. George Sand termed her contemporaries 'Sons of Prometheus' but it was remarked that she might as well have termed The Sons of Satan.[10] William Blake's 'son of fire' who fearlessly opposes the old gloomy king in his *Marriage of Heaven and Hell* is another Romantic euphemism for Lucifer, which is used similarly to 'Prometheus'.

Goethe, Byron and Shelley all wrote a poem about Prometheus. Goethe's poem is a thinly disguised address to God via Zeus, where he deeply questions the mercy and goodness of the Demiurge and paraphrases Corinthians 13:11:

When I was a child,
And did not know where from or to,
I turned my seeking eye toward
The sun, as if beyond there was
An ear to hear my complaint,
A heart like mine,
To have mercy with the embattled one.

Who helped me
Against the Titans' might?
Who saved me from Death,
From Slavery?
Did you not accomplish it all yourself,
Holy glowing Heart?
And glowed, young and good,
Deceived, thanks for salvation
To the sleeping one up there?

Shall I honour you? What for?
Have you softened the pains,
Ever, of a burdened one?
Have you silenced the tears,
Ever, of an anguished one?
Was I not forged into a Man
By almighty Time
And eternal Fate,
My masters and yours?

10 Maximilian Rudwin, ibid, p. 19.

Once again Goethe places Fate and Time as forces stronger or older than the Demiurge.

Byron's Prometheus, a generation later, is even more obviously Luciferic in its implications. Like most of his generation Byron equated Prometheus's fire from heaven not with physical fire but with a metaphorical type of fire, often depicted as lightning, that had the power of awakening the dormant intellect of man. This interest in electricity as the animating force of a new era was predictive, considering that it wouldn't be till thirty years after Byron's death and the writing of Mary Shelley's greatest work, that electricity was to begin to take the place that fire had filled for humanity for the rest of it's history—the role of light-bringer.

In the following quote one can hear Byron's resistance to the Demiurge, his allegiance with the figure of Prometheus and his celebration of this 'lightning of the mind.' Though in Byron's case he also meditated elsewhere on the negative effects an excess of this power had on many of the statesmen and prophets and other 'unquiet things', driven by purely Luciferic forces.

Essentially when Byron writes of Prometheus there is no way to tell he is not in fact writing about Lucifer and the fruit on the Tree of Knowledge.

Thy Godlike crime was to be kind,
To render with thy precepts less
The sum of human wretchedness,
And strengthen Man with his own mind;
But baffled as thou wert from high,
Still in thy patient energy,
In the endurance, and repulse
Of thine impenetrable Spirit,
Which Earth and Heaven could not convulse,
A mighty lesson we inherit:
Thou art a symbol and a sign
To Mortals of their fate and force;
Like thee, Man is in part divine.

P. B. Shelley, sharing a generation and often a location with Lord Byron, was even more radical in his *Prometheus Unbound*. We began this essay with Scudder's quote about The Prometheus, where he named it a new myth for the modern era. But what exactly makes it so new?

Firstly, Shelley's Prometheus is not only Luciferic, he heretically blends

Lucifer and Christ images together. Prometheus is explicitly a rebel against the cruel Demiurge. But rather than suffering alone like Byron's proud titan, chained to the rock, Shelley echoes Christ's crucifixion by having his punishment sympathetically witnessed by three women. Being married to the daughter of Mary Wollstonecraft, one of the first feminists, it was perhaps easier for Shelley to be cognizant of the patriarchal element of the Demiurge figure. He counters this in his 'new myth' by not only introducing a fully sympathetic Luciferic figure, but in adding a Lucifera. In fact, the figure of Asia, symbolic of feminine gnosis, must wake up before the world can be saved from the Demiurge. It is quite explicitly clear that Prometheus, our obvious Lucifer, has been separated from his female Other, and only together can they actually triumph.

This process of awaking involves an Underworld descent where Asia must encounter her own version of Das Mutters. Demorgorgon, an amorphous, genderless darkness with a voice, becomes the primeval Fate. This oracular darkness is the closest thing to a supreme authority in Shelley's poem, thus echoing Mephistopheles perspective in Goethe.

Shelley, like Byron, equates Prometheus's gift with mind fire. Shelley tells us in the poem that Prometheus gifted 'words and words gifted thought, and thought is the measure of the universe.' Thus the gift of fire, the forbidden fruit, is conveyed through the lightning of words, words that produce the Lucifer Moment, and you can't have a new thought until you've got the words to frame it.

The spirit of revolution lurks behind Shelley's Luciferic work, but he never touches on anything as close to intellectual Satanism as Byron does. It is interesting that he does so via taking Milton a step further. In Milton the figure of Lucifer decrees when he sees the hell he must endure: 'be it so'. When Byron tells us in his poem *The Dream* that:

To him the book of Night was opened wide,
And voices from the deep abyss revealed
A marvel and a secret. —Be it so.

We have not only an image of a speaking abyss, deep and dark, but the affirmation of life's poisons is spoken in direct quote of Milton's Satan's, embracing Hell as a potential Heaven when transmuted by the consciousness. Byron not only embraces the Luciferic perspective from Milton's work but puts the devil's words in his own mouth. In Byron's case this is a little more than just a literary conceit, seeing as he did in fact believe himself to be an avatar of a fallen angel.[11] Via his Childe Harold figure he also managed to equate himself with Cain and The Wandering Jew. Byron had completed the process of turning the poet into a Lucifer, a little devil, a scapegoat, and thus societies collective impulse to protect the integrity of the episteme, all trying to squash and prevent a potential Lucifer Moment, came down upon his head in condemnation.

Whilst the level of scapegoating Byron encountered during his lifetime might have been new, to equate poets with dark angels was not. As William Hazlitt famously described Coleridge's genius in *The Spirit of the Age*: 'With mighty wings outspread, his imagination might brood over the void and make it pregnant.' Here again we find the image of the dark void of formless possibility that the poets intuited was older than the Demiurge. Whilst Luciferic fire might come from the sky as mind lighting, the fecundation of the darkness by the lightning of genius became the deeper key image of the era, something far more savage seeming than the image of Abram's lamp-light.

The future lay with this new perspective on the devil. There was room for him at the edges. Victor Hugo and Lamartine both depicted the devil as somewhere between necessary for goodness and liberty to exist and actually savable.

But Victor Hugo perhaps did the best job of linking Lucifer to the spirit of revolution of his times by making Liberty Lucifer's daughter, sprouted from one of the feathers of his angel wings. The idea of Liberty, this dangerous but necessary force, characterized as feminine, much like Shelley's Lucifera figures, gives the final touch to the construction of a devil for the coming modern era.

CONCLUSION

> *More important than anything is the achievement of Romantic poetics whereby evil was brought into proximity to better be looked at.* [12]

Whether the nineteenth century poet still considered the question of Lucifer to be one of necessary evil, or was a passionate advocate that he was heroic rather than evil, the above quote is still of great significance. Be-

11 Benita Eisler, *Byron: Child of Passion, Fool of Fame,* Penguin Books, 1999, p. 454.

12 Vida D. Scudder, *op cit,* p. 22.

cause before this era, where Lucifer moved out of the theatres, ale houses and crossroads and into the literary canon, evil was something that was the province of the Other. It wasn't drawn in and looked at closely, it was laughed off or sent to the gibbet. This new willingness by the creative people of the time to accept a degree of ambiguity birthed the Byronic hero and later all the anti-hero figures that come after him.

The transformation of the ultimate transgressor into the vigilante scapegoat and sacrificial anti-hero, charts the slow dawning on behalf of the mainstream that they may have been lied to. That perhaps there is not only one master narrative being guarded for you by a benevolent elite who only wishes to keep the wolf out of your flocks. Things were made thinkable that had hitherto been unthinkable, -the glory of all true literature!

In today's world the Luciferic anti-hero is so well known that he barely causes discomfort, which is always a sign we are ready to see him in a new way very shorty. It is easier perhaps for modern westerners to embrace a darkness that does not seem so threatening, in the reign of electric light, antibiotics and touch screen communication, can the dark yawning abyss of suffering and mortality ever again seem so deep to us?

Can the Opposer, the stranger, the man at the crossroads, tinker, sailor, beggar man, thief, or travelling man, ever feel quite the threat he once did? Or will the Lucifer of this age look quite different? Or has the hidden fear of what the darkness holds only grown as our drunken obsession with false light dances dizzily near the edge? Even today powerful media-driven fear campaigns are directed towards feared minorities.

As messenger of Fate Lucifer is terrible, he is serene. But we cannot say he has nothing to do with evil for he walks every bridge as thin as a hair between all extremes, inhabits all ambiguities and grey-areas. He is hard to understand for the mind that deals in absolutes. We are an absolutist society still, a self-replicating, self-propagating monoculture that upholds one god, one life partner, one creed and old valid state of consciousness. The wakeful, buying, covertous, brightly lit screen state of consciousness seems to be steadily marching its way into tyrannically defining our episteme. What then will the modern devil look like? Who will our devils be? Who our Light Bringer? And how shall He guide us as those who attempt to wrestle ourselves out from under the control of the false light? What new master narratives will he gestate, what invisible assumptions will he violate? And in violating them draw their fragmented nature to light, holding it up against the stormy backdrop of the brooding void...

INDEX TO IMAGES BY HAGEN VON TULIEN

INDEX

CONTRIBUTORS

FRANCISCO D. was born in 1979. For the most part he taught himself how to draw, paint and experiment with innovative painting techniques through years of trial & error. He was raised in the desert and is now based outside of Seattle, Washington. Divine Mania studio is a crooked barn of creativity out in the wet countryside, where he manically paints all throughout the night, while the good world sleeps.

FREDRIK EYTZINGER is an ethnologist and occult researcher residing on the west coast of Sweden. In recent years he has been writing on subjects related to the Swedish occult milleu and magical arts, and in 2013 he released his first book entitled *Salomonic Magical Arts* with Three Hands Press. In his spare time he is also a musician and a painter, and he is a member of the international art collective Belzebez, based in Sweden.

ROBERT FITZGERALD is an initiate of the Magical Order Cultus Sabbati, and a writer researching the Thelemic Mysteries, witchcraft, and the Angelical Magic of Dr. John Dee. His first book *A Gathering of Masks* was published by Three Hands Press in 2009.

RICHARD GAVIN is a Canadian author of supernatural fiction and esotericism. His occult writings have appeared in such publications as *Starfire* journal and *Clavis: Journal of Occult Arts, Letters and Experience*. In 2016 Theion Publishing released *The Benighted Path: Primeval Gnosis and the Monstrous Soul*, Richard's book on Night Consciousness. Online presence: www.richardgavin.net

RAVEN GRIMASSI is a practicing witch and author of over 20 books on Witchcraft, Wicca, and Inner Mystery teachings. He brings over 45 years of study and practice to his work. Raven is the current directing Elder of the Ash, Birch and Willow tradition, which is a non-specific cultural system rooted in pre-Christian concepts of Witchcraft.

MICHAEL HOWARD (1948-2015) was an Anglo-Irish writer, historical researcher and editor. Since 1976 he has edited and published the witchcraft and folklore magazine *The Cauldron*. He has written 38 books on Northern European and Germanic runes, Earth Mysteries, the Luciferian tradition, the history of modern Wicca, the transition from paganism to Christianity in the British Isles, faery lore, seasonal folk customs and festivals, angelic magic, historical witches and cunning folk, modern traditional witchcraft, herbalism, and occult secret societies.

MADELEINE LEDESPENCER is a visual artist and author with a particular interest in the French decadence, fin de siècle occultism, traditional witchcraft, and Spiritualism. Her work can be found in *Dirge* Magazine, *Heathen Harvest*, and *Folk Horror Revival: Field Studies*. She is currently working on a book about the Abbé Boullan and spends her spare time as a demimondiane, absintheur, and adoratrice de Satan.

LEE MORGAN is an occultist, independent scholar and novelist living in Van Diemen's Land, Australia. Current works to date include three novels, (the most recent of which is *Unless They're Wicked*, a non-fiction introduction to the field of traditional witchcraft studies, *A Deed Without a Name*, and contributions to the Three Hands Press anthologies *Hands of Apostasy* and *Penumbrae*.

HAGEN VON TULIEN is a contemporary German artist and occultist, specializing in creating art as a manifestation of magical states of awareness, and its use as an esoteric tool. He is works in a variety of media including pen and ink, paper cut, acrylics, collage and digital formats. Currently a Master-Initiate of the Fraternitas Saturni (F.S.) and an empowered adept of the Voudon Gnostic Current.

FRATER U\D\ is a German writer, poet and magician. He is the founder of Pragmatic Magic and Ice Magic and has investigated the practical aspects of occultism in general and magic in particular for over half a century. He has written more than thirty-five books, several of which have been translated into other languages ranging from English, Spanish and Russian to Portuguese, Czech, Estonian and Japanese. He is recognized for his non-dogmatic approach to the Black Arts. Among his translations are the books of Peter Carroll and Ramsey Dukes as well as Aleister Crowley's *Book of Lies*.

ETHAN DOYLE WHITE is a doctoral candidate at University College London with research interests in both the material expressions of religiosity in early medieval England and the historical development of modern witchcraft and Paganism. He has published on these subjects in various peer-reviewed journals and is the author *of Wicca: History, Belief, and Community in Modern Pagan Witchcraft* (Sussex Academic Press, 2016)

The Luminous Stone was published at the Assumption of the Virgin, 2016 EV by Three Hands Press. This first printing is comprised of three thousand forty-nine copies in total. Of this are two thousand trade paper editions printed offset and sewn with colour covers, one thousand hardcover copies bound in green cloth with colour dust jacket; forty-nine deluxe hand-numbered copies quarter-bound in green goat and hand-marbled endpapers.

SCRIBÆ QUO MYSTERIUM FAMULATUR